Dinosaurs

Written by Dan Abnett and Nik Vincent

p

This is a Parragon Book
This edition published in 2001

Parragon
Queen Street House
4 Queen Street
Bath BA1 1HE, UK

ISBN 0 75254 818 2

Printed in Italy

Design: Matt Neal / Scott Design
Editor: Audrey Daly

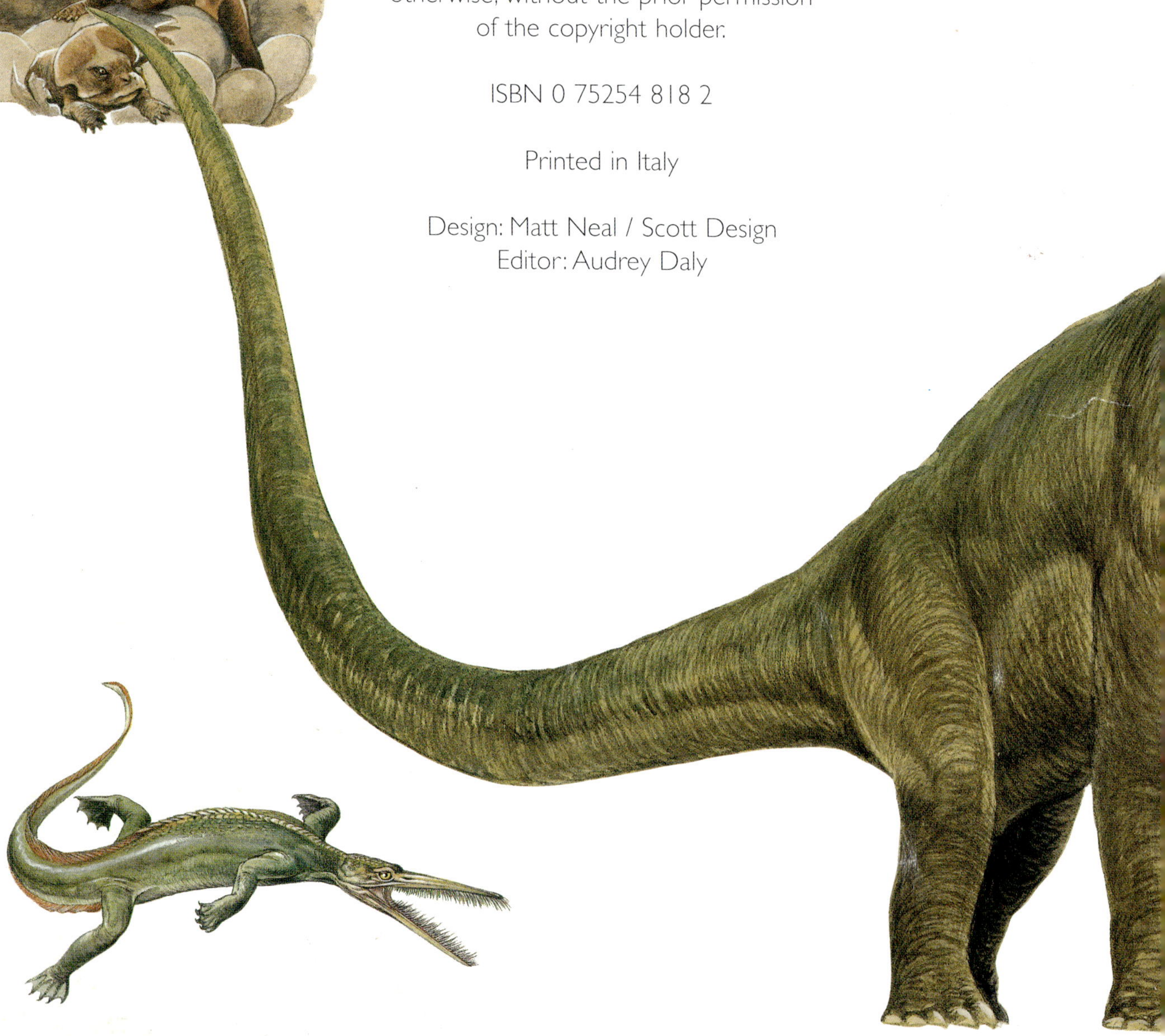

Contents

How did dinosaurs evolve?

DINOSAURS FIRST LIVED ON EARTH 230 MILLION YEARS AGO. THEY EVOLVED from reptiles, which were the first animals to live out of water all the time. All creatures before the reptiles could only live in water or, partly in water and partly on land. Reptiles lived in the Triassic period, and were like lizards with legs on the sides of their bodies. Then, over the centuries, their legs began to grow beneath their bodies, so that they could walk upright some of the time – and so, dinosaurs began to evolve.

The first animals to walk upright were called Thecodonts. They were the ancestors of the first dinosaurs. Walking upright meant that the dinosaurs could see more of what was around them, and they could run faster.

What kinds of animals did dinosaurs evolve from?

They evolved from the Thecodont, a type of archosaur which could walk upright some of the time. The Thecodonts were reptiles, and looked a bit like modern crocodiles. The Thecodonts, unlike other reptiles at that time, had legs underneath their bodies instead of at the sides.

What was an archosaur like?

Archosaur means "ruling lizard", so named because this group of reptiles was more advanced than others of its time.

To help them to swim, archosaurs had developed strong hind legs and long, strong tails. When they took to the land, this meant they could walk on their hind legs, balanced by their tails. Their short front legs had claws to catch animals, and they had sharp teeth to cut meat.

Did all the reptiles change?

One group of reptiles evolved into dinosaurs, but there were many other kinds of reptiles around at the time. Some reptiles returned to the water and some developed into other land animals, including mammals. There are still as many as 6,500 different kinds of reptiles living on Earth today, some looking very like those of dinosaur times. The name reptile comes from the Latin word meaning "to crawl".

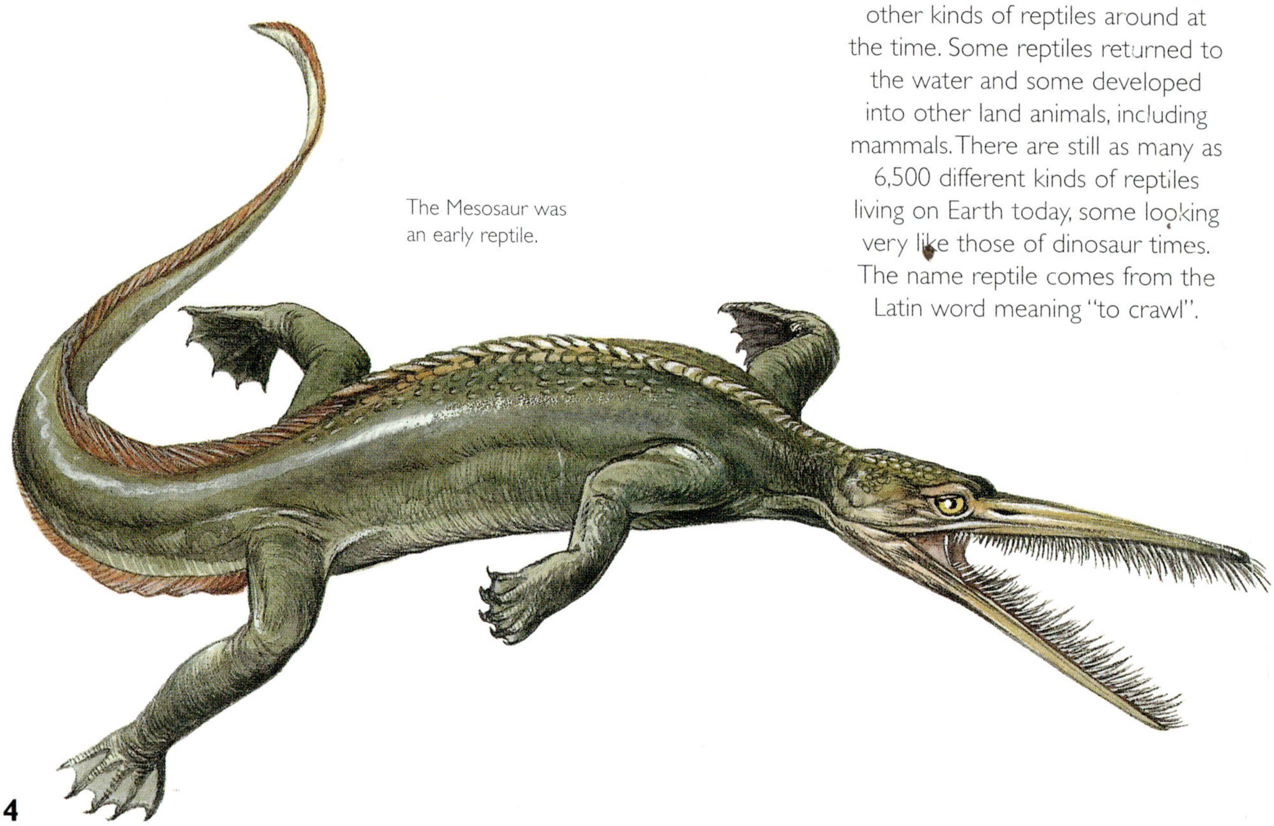

The Mesosaur was an early reptile.

How long did it take for reptiles to evolve into dinosaurs?
Evolution is a long and slow process. The first reptiles appeared during the Carboniferous period, around 340 million years ago. The first dinosaurs appeared around 100 million years later; there were a number of different types of creatures between the two time periods.

How long did the dinosaurs inhabit Earth?
The dinosaurs lived on Earth for about 165 million years. They lived all over the globe, adapting the way they lived to suit different habitats.

Did all archosaurs evolve into dinosaurs?

ALTHOUGH THE GROUP OF ARCHOSAURS CALLED THECODONTS DEVELOPED INTO dinosaurs, other archosaurs evolved into different kinds of animals or died out. Some archosaurs became pterosaurs – flying reptiles – and some developed into the crocodiles of today.

Lycaenops was a ferocious reptile that developed about the same time as the dinosaurs.

How many different kinds of dinosaurs were there?
No one knows just how many different kinds of dinosaurs there were. Some dinosaurs evolved and some became extinct, so dinosaurs changed over the millions of years they were on Earth. Scientists are still finding examples of new dinosaurs all the time, so we may never know how many types there actually were.

Where did the name dinosaur come from?
Two hundred years ago, people knew very little about dinosaurs. The word dinosaur means "terrible lizard". However, it is now known that dinosaurs were only very distantly related to lizards. And many of them were herbivores (plant-eating), so they did not fight or hunt for food.

How long have we known about dinosaurs?
The first dinosaur bones were found hundreds of years ago, but nobody knew what they were. Then about two hundred years ago, scientists began to take an interest in these strange finds, trying to work out what they might be.

How were the dinosaurs different from the Thecodonts?
The Thecodonts developed from amphibians that lived in and out of water and could walk upright some of the time. The Thecodonts didn't evolve into dinosaurs until they could walk upright all the time, giving them a better field of vision and other uses for their front legs.

Did early dinosaurs live near the water?
Dinosaurs developed from reptiles, which were the first animals that didn't need to live near water. And they were the first creatures that could lay their eggs on land instead of in the water. Dinosaurs did not need to live near water, which meant they could move all over the landmass of the Earth.

What did the first dinosaurs look like?

DINOSAURS REMIND US OF MODERN REPTILES SUCH AS CROCODILES. For millions of years, dinosaurs were the most successful animals on Earth, because they could adapt to almost any condition. Some were meat-eating and some were plant-eating, and they came in all shapes and sizes from the tiny Compsognathus to the huge Ultrasaurus at 30 metres long.

Ultrasaurus and Apatosaurus were both large plant-eating dinosaurs.

Did all dinosaurs walk upright?

The earliest dinosaurs like the Staurikosaurus and the Herrerasaurus could walk upright, but other plant-eating dinosaurs that developed walked on four legs. They had small heads but long necks, so they were still tall enough to be able to see around them.

When did the archosaurs live?

The archosaurs appeared about halfway through the Triassic period (which was between 213 and 248 million years ago). The very earliest dinosaurs evolved later in the same period.

When did the first dinosaurs appear on Earth?

The first dinosaur, Staurikosaurus, appeared about 225 or 230 million years ago, towards the end of the Triassic period, and survived for about five million years.

What were the advantages of walking upright to a dinosaur?

Reptiles before the dinosaurs could not walk upright on their back legs. This meant that they were quite slow and could not see very much above ground level. Dinosaurs' back legs were strong, so they could run faster. They could also use their front legs for gathering or hunting, or even, sometimes, for fighting.

Are there any modern animals that evolved at the same time as dinosaurs?

SOME OF OUR MODERN REPTILES LOOK LIKE DINOSAURS, AND SOME TYPES OF TURTLES began to appear at about the same time. They have changed very little in millions of years, and look just as they did in the Triassic period.

At 11 metres long, Allosaurus was one of the largest meat-eaters.

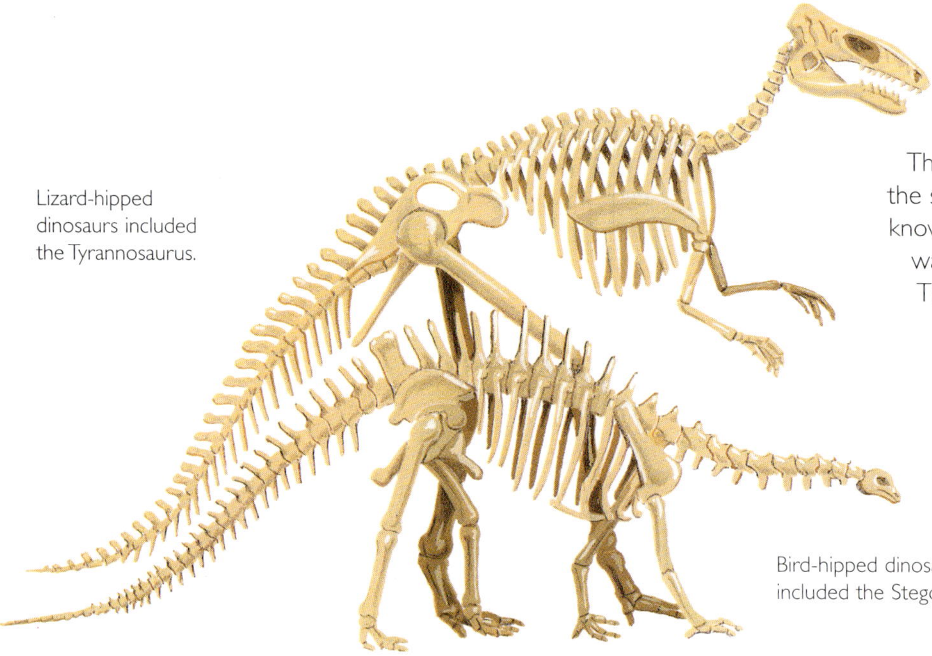

Lizard-hipped dinosaurs included the Tyrannosaurus.

Bird-hipped dinosaurs included the Stegosaurus.

What were the two types of dinosaurs?

THERE WERE TWO MAIN TYPES OF DINOSAURS. THE MOST IMPORTANT difference between the two is in the shape of their hip joints. Dinosaurs with pelvic or hipbones like lizards are called Saurischia. This group includes both meat-eating dinosaurs and the huge four-legged plant-eating dinosaurs. Dinosaurs in the second group are called Ornithischia, and are those with pelvic or hipbones more like birds. All bird-hipped dinosaurs were plant-eating, and were smaller than the plant-eating sauropods.

When did the two types of dinosaur appear?
They appeared on Earth at about the same time, although the earliest known dinosaur, the Staurikosaurus, was a lizard-hipped Saurischian. The bird-hipped dinosaurs are almost as old as the oldest lizard-hipped dinosaurs.

Were all the dinosaurs related?
All dinosaurs appear to have evolved from the Thecodonts. Some scientists however, think that they must have developed from slightly different creatures, since some have lizard hips and some have bird hips.

Were there groups of dinosaurs within these two main groups?
The Saurischian dinosaurs can be divided into two groups. The theropods walked upright and were meat-eaters. The sauropods were plant-eaters and walked on four legs. They had long necks, and most of them were gigantic. The Ornisthician dinosaurs were all plant-eaters, but could also be divided into two groups. The fabrosaurs had non-grinding teeth and the heterodontosaurs had grinding teeth.

The Heterodontosaurus was one of the earliest bird-hipped dinosaurs.

Why did the plant-eating sauropods walk on four legs?
Many sauropods were meat-eaters and walked on two legs, but large plant-eating dinosaurs needed bigger stomachs. Meat is rich in goodness, but plant-eating dinosaurs had to eat a lot more to get the same amount of goodness from their food.
The plant-eating sauropods had bigger stomachs so they couldn't balance properly on two legs. They had to walk on four legs.

The Compsognathus was only about 70 centimetres long. It ate insects and lizards.

How big were the dinosaurs?
One of the largest known dinosaurs was the lizard-hipped Ultrasaurus, which ate plants. It was 30 metres long and, with its long neck, it stood taller than a modern three-storey house. Some of the smaller dinosaurs such as the Compsognathus were less than a metre long.

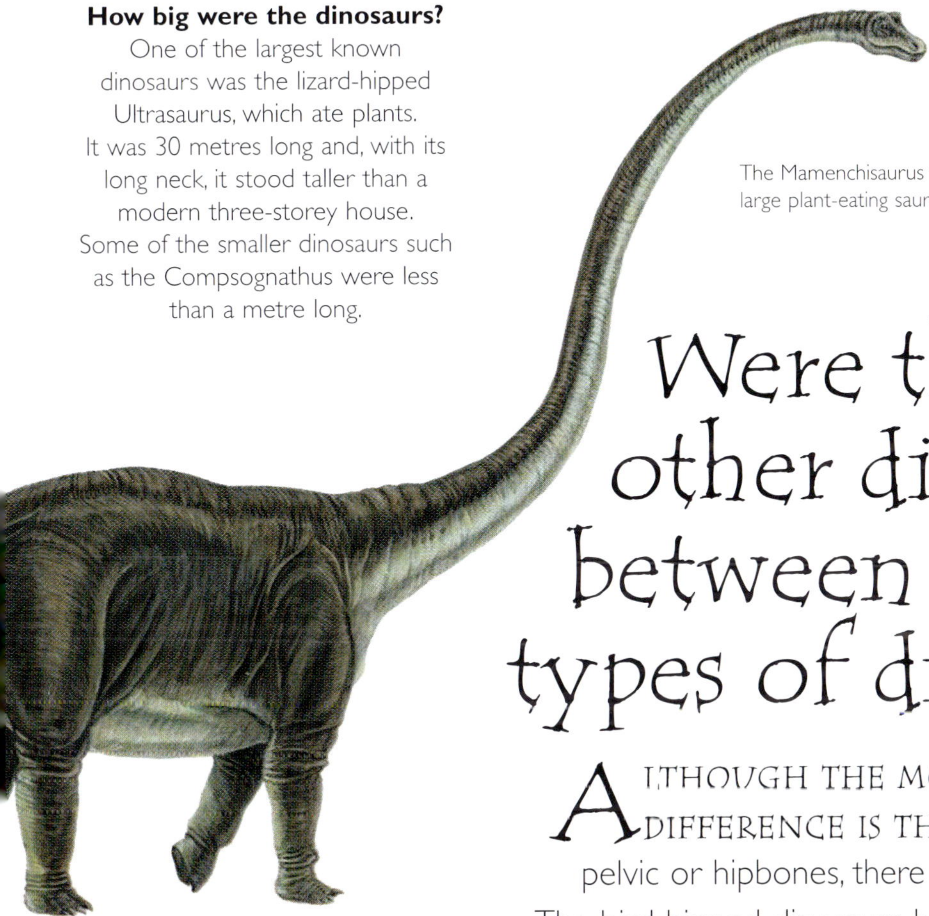

The Mamenchisaurus was another large plant-eating sauropod.

Were there any other differences between the two types of dinosaurs?

ALTHOUGH THE MOST OBVIOUS DIFFERENCE IS THE SHAPE OF THEIR pelvic or hipbones, there are other differences. The bird-hipped dinosaurs have a bone at the end of their lower jaw, but the lizard-hipped dinosaurs don't have this. The two types also have different kinds of teeth. Bird-hips have strengthened backbones, too, which look different from those of lizard-hipped ones. No evidence has been found to show that one type of dinosaur evolved from the other and, because of the differences between them, scientists believe they evolved from different kinds of creatures.

Was one type of dinosaur more successful than the other?
Both the Saurischia and the Ornisthicia evolved and changed throughout the age of the dinosaurs, but they both continued in their different forms until the dinosaurs became extinct. There is no evidence to suggest that one group took over or was more successful than the other.

What was the Triassic period?

THE TRIASSIC PERIOD WAS A TIME IN EARTH'S HISTORY BETWEEN 248 AND 213 million years ago. Earth looked very different then. All the land of the world was joined together in one piece, not separated by seas and oceans as it is today. The landmass of the Triassic period is called the Panagaea. The land was different because there were no grasses or flowers. The plants were mostly conifers, like fir trees and ferns of all kinds. The weather was also much drier than it is now.

Earth looked very different (1) 200 million years (2) 100 million years ago to how it looks today (3).

What does Triassic mean?

Scientists have given the name Triassic (from trias, meaning three) to the three-layered rock system in which the remains of the first dinosaurs have been found. The Triassic period was followed by the Jurassic period.

What were the first dinosaurs?

Two of the very earliest dinosaurs were small meat-eaters. The Herrerasaurus and the Staurikosaurus were only 2 or 3 metres long and walked upright. Little is known about these Saurischians, but the Staurikosaurus had long back legs and probably moved quite quickly. The Herrerasaurus was heavier, with a large head and strong jaws.

Two of the earliest dinosaurs were Herrerasaurus and Staurikosaurus.

Where did the first dinosaurs live?

Although the earliest dinosaur remains were found in South America, this does not mean that the first dinosaurs came from there. During the Triassic period, South America was joined to Africa.

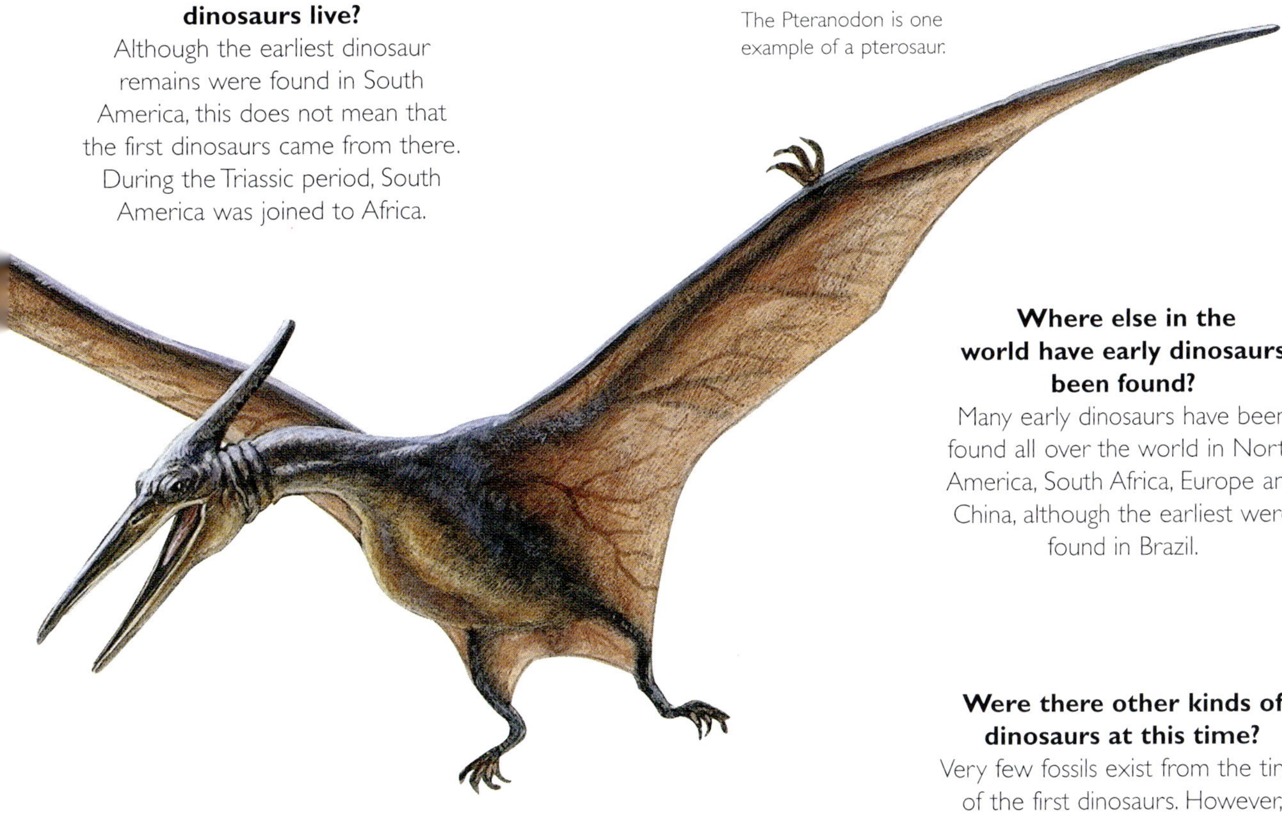

The Pteranodon is one example of a pterosaur.

Where else in the world have early dinosaurs been found?

Many early dinosaurs have been found all over the world in North America, South Africa, Europe and China, although the earliest were found in Brazil.

Were there other kinds of dinosaurs at this time?

Very few fossils exist from the time of the first dinosaurs. However, there is evidence that there were other creatures that were evolving into dinosaurs at this time.

What other kinds of animals existed in the Triassic period?

DURING THE TRIASSIC PERIOD, WHEN THE DINOSAURS FIRST APPEARED, THERE WERE all kinds of creatures both on land and in the water. The earliest mammals, warm-blooded creatures with hair or fur, appeared at about the same time as dinosaurs. Dinosaurs were stronger and better adapted to conditions, however, so many of the earliest mammals soon died out. But after the dinosaurs themselves became extinct, mammals took over as the most successful animals on Earth.

Were there animals in the water?

Many water creatures continued to thrive in the seas and oceans of Earth, including reptiles that lived partly on the land. Eventually, these sorts of reptiles died out, however, the smaller crocodiles and turtles still exist today.

Were there any birds?

The first flying animals appeared over 200 million years ago. They were more like flying reptiles than birds, and were called pterosaurs. The pterosaurs ruled the skies while the dinosaurs ruled the land.

What does Jurassic mean?
The Jurassic period is recognised by layers of rock in the ground at a different level from the Triassic. These layers are made of the same type of rock as the Jura mountains and that is how they got the name Jurassic.

What was the Jurassic period?

THE JURASSIC PERIOD WAS A TIME IN EARTH'S HISTORY BETWEEN 213 AND 144 million years ago. It is probably the most famous period of dinosaur history, because it was then that dinosaurs became the dominant land animals. The continents of Earth were still very close together, so the dinosaurs were able to roam and spread all over the world. This was the time of the really huge dinosaurs like the Ultrasaurus.

The Megalosaurus or "great lizard" was a meat-eating dinosaur found in the UK. It was 9 metres long.

How had the dinosaurs developed?
Since dinosaurs didn't have other animals to compete with, they were able to develop and adapt to the climate and landscape of Earth unhindered. They became the most successful of the land animals. There was an abundance of food for the plant-eating dinosaurs, which meant that there were plenty of plant-eating dinosaurs to provide meat for the larger meat-eating dinosaurs.

How did dinosaurs evolve to cope with their size?
The largest dinosaurs were the biggest land animals ever seen on Earth, and to accommodate their huge size they had to evolve in certain ways. One way was that their skeletons had to become very strong to support their huge bulk.

How was Earth changing?
By the end of the Jurassic period, the landmass known as the Panagaea had begun to split up and separate into continents. But land bridges between these new continents meant that the dinosaurs could still move wherever they wanted to. There was more rain at this time and plants were plentiful.
As the Jurassic period was ending, the first flowering plants had started to appear.

Allosaurus was an early relative of the huge Tyrannosaurus.

How large were the dinosaurs from the Jurassic period?

Diplodocus was a 27 metre long plant-eating dinosaur and Allosaurus, an 11 metre long meat-eater, but the biggest of the plant-eaters was the Brachiosaurus, and the biggest meat-eater was Megalosaurus Ingens.

What other animals existed during the Jurassic period?

The only animals on Earth at this time that were more than a metre long were all dinosaurs. There were also tiny mammals and of course insects, but Earth was certainly dominated by dinosaurs of all kinds. Surprisingly, no dinosaurs ever learned to live in the seas and oceans of the world, nor did they learn to fly. They were very well adapted to the land and never ventured from it.

Were the sea creatures changing?

The seas swarmed with fish of all kinds, which were beginning to look more and more like the fish we know today. There were also ammonites, which are now extinct. Meat-eating reptiles called ichthyosaurs and plesiosaurs still inhabited the seas, preying on the fish.

The Archaeopteryx – the very first bird.

Were there any birds?

THE SKIES HAD BEEN CONTROLLED BY THE FLYING REPTILES CALLED PTEROSAURS UNTIL the first birds began to appear at the end of the Jurassic period. The first known bird is called Archaeopteryx. It was a long time, however, before the pterosaurs became extinct and modern birds took over.

The Shonisaurus was the largest ichthyosaur. It was 15 metres long.

What does Cretaceous mean?
The Cretaceous period was named after the chalk layers where dinosaurs remains from this time are found. Cretaceous simply means chalky.

The Tyrannosaurus was one of the last new dinosaurs.

What was the Cretaceous period?

THE CRETACEOUS PERIOD WAS A TIME IN EARTH'S HISTORY FROM 144 TO 65 MILLION years ago. It was the last period in which there were dinosaurs on Earth. By the end of this time they were extinct. Chalk beds were forming on Earth then, and this age is named after them.

Which dinosaurs did well during the Cretaceous period?
The successful stegosaurs and sauropods were common dinosaurs during the Jurassic period, but began to die out and become isolated during the Cretaceous. Ankylosaurs had been around during the Jurassic period, and flourished during the Cretaceous. This suggests that they were better able to cope with the changes in the Earth at this time. The mighty Tyrannosaurs also did well then, living in Asia and North America.

How was the Earth changing?
Earth continued to change. The landmasses were moving further and further apart, becoming islands with seas around them. Plants also began to change – there were more and more flowering plants that couldn't grow all year round. The Earth began to have seasons, which meant colder winters and warmer summers.

How did the changing world affect the dinosaurs?
Changes in the landmass of the Earth meant that the dinosaurs became trapped between the seas and couldn't move around so easily. The changes in plants meant a lack of food for the plant-eating dinosaurs, and the new seasons meant that dinosaurs had to adapt to heat and cold in order to survive. All these changes may be why the dinosaurs began to die out.

Did some Cretaceous dinosaurs flourish throughout the world?
The Iguanodons also did well during this period and their fossils have been found all over the world. It is unusual for the later dinosaurs to be so widespread because the landmass of Earth was breaking up and seas and oceans were separating the continents. It appears that the Iguanodons managed to find land routes all over the world, even travelling from America across Antarctica and into Australia.

What other animals existed during the Cretaceous period?

Morganucodon was a small early mammal.

MAMMALS AND LIZARDS CONTINUED TO LIVE ALONGSIDE THE DINOSAURS, AND snakes began to appear for the first time. The mammals were still small, and the lizards lived in the wet areas of land. The dinosaurs went on dominating Earth right to the end of their existence. No other animals grew so huge or adapted so well to the conditions of the time.

How had the dinosaurs developed?

The dinosaurs began to live in smaller areas of land separated by seas and oceans. This meant that they couldn't move around as much. Some managed to develop and change, but others couldn't adapt and died out.

New dinosaurs had to evolve to keep up with the changing world. The Tyrannosaurus was one of the last of the new dinosaurs. It was 12 metres long and a meat-eater. It was found in Canada and the USA.

How were flying animals developing?

Pterosaurs were still ruling the skies, but the first bird had begun to evolve. By the end of the Cretaceous period, there were lots of different birds, very similar to the birds known today. Some of the birds of the time, however, still had teeth.

Did the first birds develop from the pterosaurs?

Scientists believe that the first bird, Archaeopteryx, was closely related to the dinosaurs. It had many similar features to the reptiles. Although Archaeopteryx was a winged bird, it also had clawed fingers, a bony tail and even teeth. The first bird may not have been very good at flying, but probably climbed trees and then launched itself into flight from high branches.

Kronosaurus was a reptile that lived in the water and ate fish.

How were the sea creatures developing?

Fish continued to evolve throughout this time. The reptiles that preyed on the fish began to change, resembling the monitor lizards of today. They were called mosasaurs.

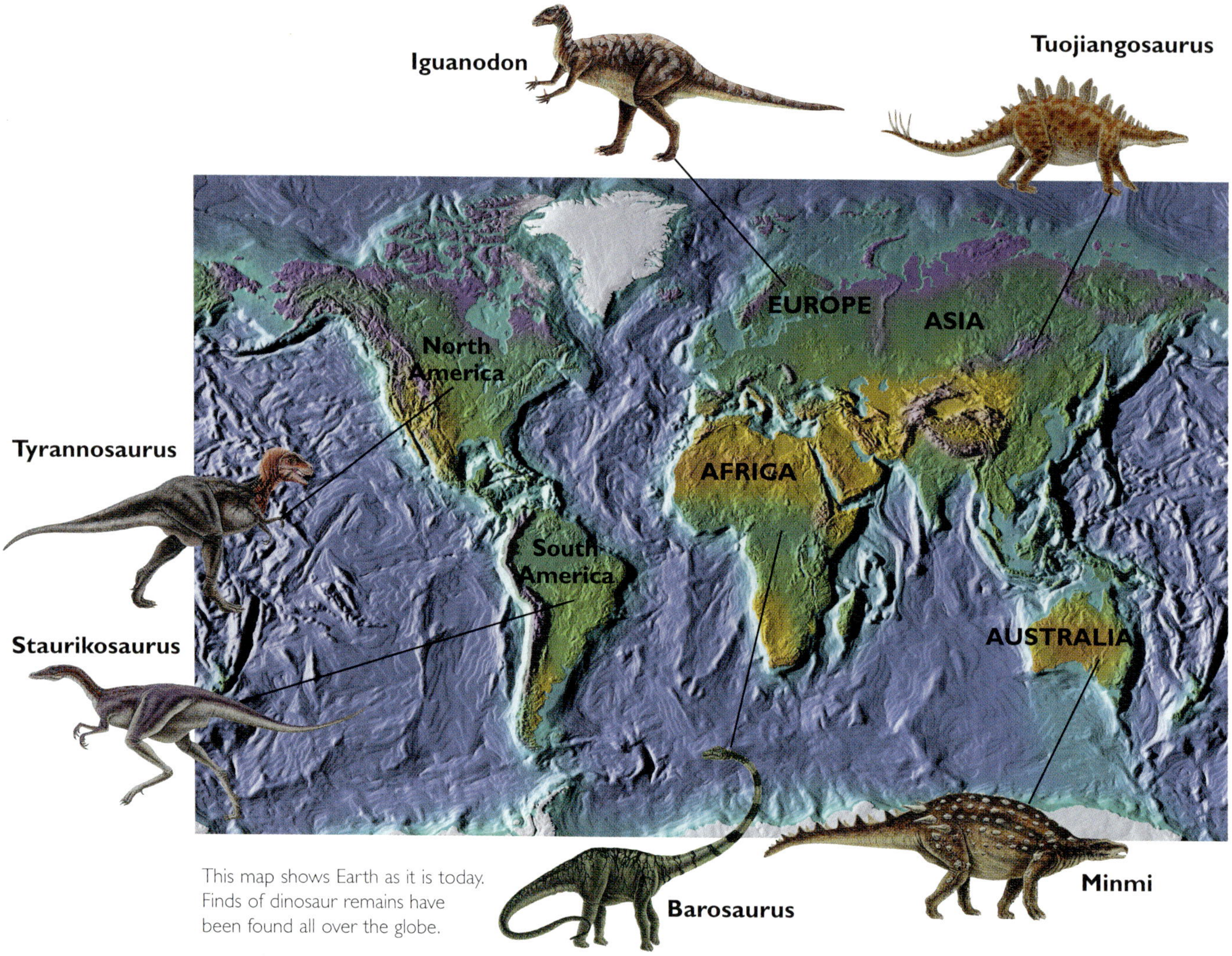

This map shows Earth as it is today. Finds of dinosaur remains have been found all over the globe.

Where in the world did the dinosaurs live?

DINOSAURS LIVED ON EARTH FOR MILLIONS OF YEARS AND THEY SAW THEIR PLANET change enormously throughout the three long periods of Earth's history that have already been mentioned. The dinosaurs lived on land and when they first appeared, at the end of the Triassic period, all the land on Earth was joined together in one piece.

What was the Panagaea?
The earliest dinosaurs lived in a world where all the land was in one place. When they wanted to roam, they didn't need to cross water to travel great distances. The remains of the earliest dinosaurs have been found in places that are now oceans apart, but in the Triassic period were once part of the same piece of land, known as the Panagaea.

Were there continents on the Earth?
When the continents began to form and move away from one another, the dinosaurs became isolated. Some of the later dinosaurs have each been found in only one small area because they didn't have great landmasses to walk across.

Have dinosaurs been found in Great Britain?

There have been some important discoveries of dinosaur bones in Great Britain. 180 years ago a scientist called Gideon Mantell found Megalosaurus bones in Sussex in England. He was one of the earliest palaeontologists to study dinosaur bones in Britain.

Are dinosaur bones still being found in Great Britain?

Dinosaur bones are still being found in Britain, particularly in the Isle of Wight, where some of the first Iguanodon bones were discovered – this island is particularly rich in dinosaur finds.

What kinds of new dinosaurs are being found?

In China, over the last few years, many new dinosaurs have been discovered and scientists are still working to find out exactly what they are. The new finds include dinosaurs that were probably covered in feathers.

The Iguanodon has been found on the Isle of Wight.

The Minmi has been found only in Australia.

Who were the dinosaur collectors?

The Dinosaur National Monument in Utah, USA.

DINOSAURS ARE KNOWN ABOUT TODAY BECAUSE OF THE PEOPLE WHO HAVE found actual dinosaur remains. In the USA there is a place called the Dinosaur National Monument where dinosaur bones were being dug up over a hundred years ago. Dinosaur hunters have found bones all over North and South America, Africa, Europe, Asia and even Australia.

Did the same kinds of dinosaur live all over the world?

Similar types of early dinosaurs have been found all over the world. The later dinosaurs, which were isolated in smaller areas of land, are found in fewer places.

Although the Tyrannosaurus and Tarbosaurus must have been related, they evolved differently because they lived on opposite sides of the world.

What did the dinosaurs eat?

The Struthiomimus was an omnivore.

MOST DINOSAURS WERE EITHER MEAT-EATERS OR PLANT-EATERS. Meat-eaters are called carnivores and plant-eaters are called herbivores, and nearly all dinosaurs were either one or the other. There were however, some omnivores – animals that ate both plants and meat. The Struthiomimus was one of these. It looked something like an ostrich, and ate plants as well as insects and lizards.

The meat-eating Tyrannosaurus would attack other dinosaurs for food.

What did meat-eating dinosaurs look like?

Meat-eating dinosaurs walked on their back legs, and were strong and fast. They had short necks and large heads with powerful jaws, making it easier for them to catch and kill their food.

Meat-eaters came in all sizes. The Compsognathus was small, less than a metre long. It was very fast with sharp teeth. The most famous dinosaurs are the big meat-eating dinosaurs which grew to over ten metres long.

What did plant-eaters look like?

The largest plant-eating dinosaurs – the sauropods – walked on four legs and were the biggest of all. They could grow to more than thirty metres long. They had small heads and long necks which meant they could reach food high up in trees. Smaller plant-eaters like the Lesothosaurus could walk or run on two legs. This dinosaur grew to one or two metres and grazed near the ground.

How did the meat-eaters catch their food?

There were many different meat-eating dinosaurs, but some were very specialised.

The Oviraptor, for example, may have eaten eggs, which it scooped up in its three-fingered claws and broke open with its strong jaws.

What was the largest meat-eating dinosaur?
Before Tyrannosaurus the Allosaurus was the largest meat-eater. It was 11 metres long. Like the later Tyrannosaurus, it had adapted to attacking smaller dinosaurs. It was very strong and could judge distances very well.

The Oviraptor probably ate eggs.

Spinosaurus was a 15 metre long meat-eater.

What kinds of animals did the meat-eating dinosaurs feed on?
The largest meat-eating dinosaurs would prey on other dinosaurs, hunting and killing them. Smaller meat-eaters however, could not possibly attack bigger dinosaurs so they would feed on insects, lizards and the few small mammals that were on Earth at that time. Many of these mammals were not much bigger than mice and could easily be caught and eaten by the smaller meat-eating dinosaurs.

How did the plant-eaters feed?

THE LARGEST OF THE HERBIVORE DINOSAURS MUST HAVE SPENT ALMOST ALL THEIR TIME eating. They had to eat an enormous amount of food to become so huge. The Diplodocus was 27 metres long, with a long neck to feed from high branches and a very long tail. The large plant-eating dinosaurs had to walk on four feet because of their huge stomachs.

The skeleton of a Diplodocus.

How did the smaller plant-eaters feed?
Some of the herbivores could be as small as a cat and so couldn't reach high into trees to feed. At this time, the Earth was covered in low-growing plants like ferns, so the smaller plant-eating dinosaurs had plenty to eat at ground level.

What kinds of plants did dinosaurs eat?
Nearly all through the time the dinosaurs were alive, there were no flowering plants. Most of the plants were like our modern conifers with leaves shaped like needles and grew all year round. There were also smaller plants like ferns and horsetails – plants that can still be seen today. Many of the plants had hard waxy leaves.

Were they warm-blooded or cold-blooded?

COLD-BLOODED ANIMALS CANNOT KEEP THEIR BODIES WARM WITH ENERGY FROM FOOD. They are warmed by the sun and go cold when it is dark. Warm-blooded animals keep their body at one temperature all the time. They do this by using the energy from their food to keep them warm.

At 3 metres long, the Komodo dragon is the largest modern lizard.

Were dinosaurs cold-blooded?
Scientists thought that dinosaurs were like reptiles, so they thought they also must have been cold-blooded. Scientists have been looking at the evidence again however, and are no longer sure that this is true.

What does it mean to be cold-blooded?
Modern reptiles are cold-blooded. When they become cold, these animals slow down, which can happen at night or during the colder seasons of the year. As soon as a cold-blooded animal cannot move quickly, he is in danger from predators. But dinosaurs do not appear to have slowed down as modern lizards have done, since many of them were hunters and had to be able to move quickly.

Plant-eaters like the Lufengosaurus must have eaten a huge amount of food if they were cold-blooded.

Were some of the dinosaurs cold-blooded?

Scientists don't know if the largest plant-eating animals were warm or cold-blooded. Warm-blooded animals need to eat more than cold-blooded ones to keep themselves warm. If these huge dinosaurs were warm-blooded, they would have had to eat a massive amount of food to keep their bodies warm, so they may have been cold-blooded.

Were some dinosaurs warm-blooded?

Some scientists believe that the long-necked dinosaurs must have been warm-blooded. If they were cold-blooded, these dinosaurs would not have had a high enough blood pressure for blood to reach their brains.

Is there any other evidence to show whether dinosaurs were warm or cold-blooded?

The bony plates on some dinosaurs' backs might have evolved to trap the sun's heat and warm their bodies. These dinosaurs were possibly cold-blooded.

The plates on the back of the Tuojiangosaurus may have helped him to keep warm if he was cold-blooded.

What does the evidence show?

THERE IS SOME EVIDENCE THAT DINOSAURS MIGHT HAVE BEEN COLD-BLOODED AND some evidence that they might have been warm-blooded. Nobody knows for certain. There were probably examples of both kinds.

Will we ever know whether dinosaurs were warm or cold-blooded?

Scientists are still working to find out more about dinosaurs – what they looked like, and whether they were warm or cold-blooded. New discoveries are being made all the time, and new dinosaurs are being found. As more and more evidence is gathered, there is a greater chance of finding out just what these creatures were like. Perhaps one day we will know all the answers.

Did dinosaurs live in herds?

SCIENTISTS HAVE LOOKED AT FOOTPRINTS MADE BY DINOSAURS MILLIONS OF YEARS AGO. These fossils show that some dinosaurs moved around in herds. They lived in groups of sometimes a hundred or more animals. They travelled and lived together. Some of them even hunted in packs.

How do we know which dinosaurs lived in herds?
The Apatosaurus was one of the largest plant-eating dinosaurs that lived in herds. This is known because the Apatosaurus' fossilised footprints found in North America were all made at the same time.

The huge Apatosaurus could probably walk at about the speed of a modern elephant – about 15 miles an hour.

What were the advantages of living in a herd?
The dinosaurs that lived in herds were often plant-eaters, and some of them would have been in danger from meat-eating dinosaurs. So it was probably safer for these dinosaurs to live in groups. Some dinosaur tracks have smaller footprints in the middle of the pack. This shows that the smaller and younger dinosaurs walked in the middle of the herd, protected by the larger, adult dinosaurs around them.

Did dinosaur herds travel?
Dinosaurs could move very freely around the Earth while all the landmasses were still joined together. Dinosaur herds had to travel to find food because if they always fed in one place, the food would soon become scarce. So they travelled around, sometimes large distances, to find new sources of food.

This photograph shows dinosaur footprints found in Queensland, Australia.

What kinds of dinosaurs lived in herds?

MOST OF THE HERDING DINOSAURS WERE HERBIVORES, INCLUDING THE LARGE sauropods. The horned dinosaurs, the cerotopsians and the duck-billed dinosaurs are also thought to have lived in herds, so that they could graze safely. Predators would have found it more difficult to hunt them if they lived in groups.

What kinds of dinosaurs lived alone?
Meat-eating dinosaurs were more likely to live alone. They had to be able to move fast to catch their food, and this would have been difficult in a herd. Dinonycus was a meat-eating dinosaur that may have hunted in small packs, but would never have formed part of a large herd like the plant-eaters.

Did the balloons and crests on dinosaurs' heads have a purpose?
Some dinosaurs had crests and balloons on their heads. Scientists think that these may have been used like amplifiers, to make the dinosaurs' noises louder. This would help the dinosaur to warn other members of its herd of dangers.

The Parasaurolophus and Saurolophus were dinosaurs that had crests on their heads.

The name Triceratops means "three-horned face" because of the dinosaur's head armour.

What were the plates and crests?

MANY DINOSAURS HAD ALL KINDS OF ADORNMENTS TO THEIR HEADS AND bodies, including plates, spines, helmets, crests, horns and spikes. Some of these were hard and bony, others were hollow and quite fragile, but they must all have evolved for a reason. Scientists have come up with a number of different ideas why dinosaurs might have developed these extra body parts.

Did the dinosaurs have armour?
The large meat-eating dinosaurs would eat other dinosaurs that were smaller or badly protected. So many of the slower moving plant-eaters grew armour to protect themselves. Some grew protection on their heads and some on their bodies or tails as a form of defence.

How was head armour used?
Dinosaurs like Triceratops and Styracosaurus had armoured heads, with horns and spikes on them. The horns on the heads of these dinosaurs were used for self defence. Scientists now think that the Triceratops probably also fought one another.

The Pachycephalosaurus had a very hard head.

Were there other types of head armour?
The Pachycephalosaurus had a large, thick domed skull which was a form of head armour. It could head-butt anything that might attack it.

How was body armour used?
Other dinosaurs had body protection. The Edmontonia from the Cretaceous period was a plant-eating dinosaur that walked on all fours. Its body was covered in plates of defensive armour and its skull was thick. The Edmontonia would have been too slow to get away from a predator, so its armour would help it to survive an attack.

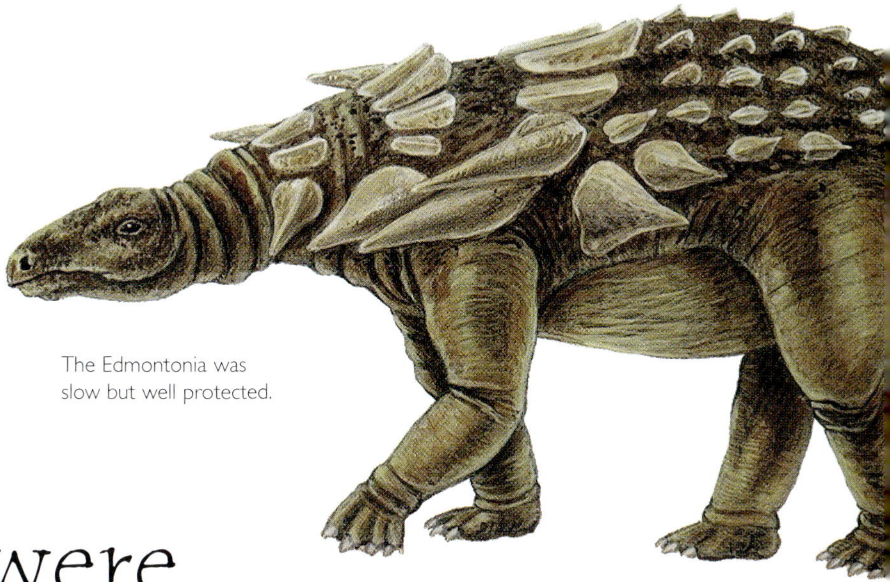
The Edmontonia was slow but well protected.

How were plates used?

STEGOSAURUS HAD PLATES ALONG ITS BACK. IT WAS THOUGHT AT ONE TIME THAT THESE were a form of armour, but new evidence shows that this was unlikely. The hard spikes and horns seen on other dinosaurs probably were armour, but the plates on a Stegosaurus were different. To begin with, they were not well placed for defence. And they were not very deeply rooted in the body, so they would fall off before they could do any damage to another dinosaur. Scientists now believe that these plates may have been used like solar panels to keep the dinosaur's body warm.

Did dinosaurs use weapons?
Some of the dinosaurs didn't just have defensive armour. The Euoplocephalus had bony spines all over its back, but it also had a clubbed tail to use as a weapon.

The Euoplocephalus could swing its tail to attack.

The Stegosaurus was a plant-eater about 7 metres long.

Were there other reasons why dinosaurs had these adornments?
Some dinosaurs like Lambeosaurus or Corythosaurus had strange crests on their heads. These are too fragile to have been any use as defence or for head-butting. They may simply have been ornaments to attract other dinosaurs for mating.

How did dinosaurs reproduce?

DINOSAURS HAVE MORE IN COMMON WITH REPTILES THAN any other modern animals, so it is not surprising that they reproduced in a similar way to reptiles. Female dinosaurs laid eggs, which had leathery shells for protection. Some dinosaurs made nests in the mud in the way that modern crocodiles do.

The Protoceratops probably protected its young.

What did the eggs look like?
It is nearly 80 years since the first dinosaur eggs were found in the Gobi desert in Mongolia. They looked very much like ordinary eggs. The eggs of some dinosaurs were round and others were oval, like modern birds' eggs. Surprisingly, the eggs were not as big as you might think. The biggest ones found are only about 30 centimetres long, which seems small when you remember how big some of the dinosaurs were.

Did male and female dinosaurs look different?
In many species of modern animals the males and females look slightly different. No one is quite sure if the same is true for dinosaurs. Scientists have found two slightly different types of the same dinosaur and think these may have been the male and female. It is possible, of course, that males and females were different in their colouring, but very little is known about what colour they were. They could have been any colour at all.

How did scientists find out about dinosaur reproduction?
Scientists have found fossils of eggs and nests and even of hatchlings, so they know this is how the dinosaurs reproduced. Although many single nests have been found, some were close together, in groups.

Did herding dinosaurs nest together?
The giant sauropods, who lived in herds, also nested in herds creating a nursery. The titanosaurs dug nests like shallow sandpits – groups of these nests have been found in India.

How did dinosaurs make nests?
Some of the dinosaur nests were probably just trampled or scooped areas of earth or sand, which would have been easy to make. Nests were sometimes also covered, and dinosaurs may have used their smaller front legs to move earth or sand, or gather and spread plants, to achieve this.

Did dinosaurs take care of their young?

SINCE DINOSAUR EGGS WERE SO SMALL, DINOSAUR BABIES MUST HAVE BEEN VERY small as well. They probably needed looking after for some time until they grew up and could look after themselves. For example, dinosaur parents may have helped their young to feed. And dinosaur footprints have been found which make it clear that smaller dinosaurs travelled along with the adults and may have been looked after by the herd.

Were dinosaurs good parents?
Scientists believe that the Maiasaura dinosaur was a very good mother. The word Maiasaura itself means "good mother lizard". This dinosaur built large mud nests and laid about twenty eggs no more than 20 centimetres long. The eggs were then covered to protect them and keep them warm.

Maiasaura took great care of her eggs and young.

When did the dinosaur age end?

THE DINOSAURS DIED OUT COMPLETELY ABOUT 65 MILLION YEARS AGO, BUT NOBODY really knows why. The dinosaurs had been the most successful land animals in the world for about 165 million years, but suddenly their age on Earth ended. Dinosaurs did not die out gradually over a long period of time, in the way other animals have done, and they do not seem to have evolved into any of the animals we see today. Scientists have been trying for a long time to find out why the dinosaurs suddenly became extinct.

Saltasaurus was one of the last known dinosaurs.

How much had the Earth changed during the dinosaur age?

During the long age of the dinosaurs, Earth changed a great deal. The land split into continents, with oceans and seas between them. The climate changed, bringing more rain and more tropical areas. Vegetation evolved, too, so that instead of just conifers and ferns, flowering plants began to grow. The years also began to have seasons for the first time.

Why did the dinosaurs become extinct?

The dinosaurs may have simply died out. It may have been partly because they could not evolve fast enough to keep up with the changing world. Throughout the Triassic, Jurassic and Cretaceous periods, dinosaurs evolved into new kinds of dinosaurs. Some also became extinct. It is, however, strange that all the dinosaurs should have died out at the same time.

Earth may have been covered in dust and smoke when the dinosaurs became extinct.

Was there a disaster?

There may have been some kind of disaster at the end of the Cretaceous period, which caused the dinosaurs to die out. This is called an extinction event. There could have been many reasons for a disaster to occur on the Earth at this time. For example, a huge rock from outer space could have hit the planet very hard. That rock might have been a meteor, a comet or an asteroid and may have made a vast crater on the planet, causing a huge amount of dust to be thrown out into the Earth's atmosphere. This might have been followed by widespread fires across the globe.

What happens to the Earth during an extinction event?

IF A CATASTROPHE DID HAPPEN AND THE EARTH WAS COVERED IN DUST AND SMOKE for a long time, this would have blocked out the sun. And without the sun to warm the Earth, plants would have died. The plant-eating dinosaurs would have had nothing to eat. When the herbivores had died, the meat-eating dinosaurs would have had nothing to eat, and so all of them would soon have become extinct. This is just one possible explanation.

Did other creatures become extinct at the same time as the dinosaurs?

All the dinosaurs became extinct at the end of the Cretaceous period, but there were other animals that disappeared at the same time.

Reptiles, like the pterosaurs in the skies and the mosasaurs and plesiosaurs in the water, also died off. At the same time, some of the tiniest creatures of the Earth and seas also disappeared.

Did any of these creatures have anything in common with dinosaurs?

All the animals that became extinct at the same time had one thing in common with the dinosaurs.

Dinosaurs needed a warm environment that didn't change very much, and the other animals that died out also had to have this kind of climate. From this, scientists are fairly sure that the climate must have changed dramatically to cause the extinction of so many different kinds of creatures.

What might have happened if the dinosaurs had not died out?

No one will ever know for sure what would have happened if the dinosaurs had survived.

Man is a mammal, and it was not until after the dinosaurs became extinct and the Earth had changed that man began to evolve.

Some scientists think that the small mammals, like mice, that lived during the age of the dinosaurs, would never have changed, and that man would never have existed.

What is palaeontology?

WHEN THE FIRST DINOSAUR BONES WERE FOUND ABOUT TWO HUNDRED YEARS AGO, no one had any idea what the animals might have been or when they had lived. Scientists began to study them. People who discover and study fossils are called palaeontologists. For the last 140 years they have been trying to find out as much as they can about creatures who lived on Earth a long time ago, including, of course, dinosaurs.

Who were the first palaeontologists?
It was only about two hundred years ago that dinosaurs were recognised as extinct reptiles of some kind. In 1841 a man called Sir Richard Owen first gave them the name dinosaurs.

Sir Richard Owen

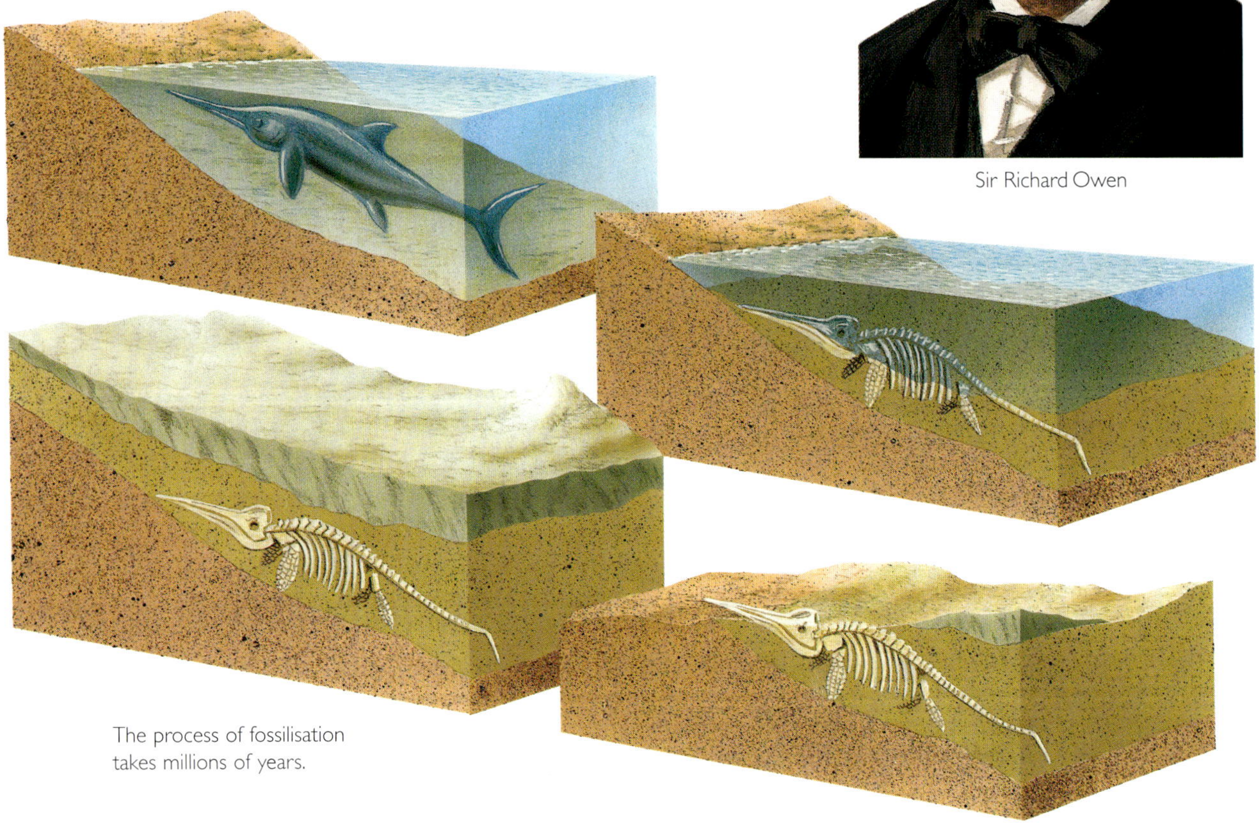

The process of fossilisation takes millions of years.

How were the different dinosaurs named?
Once dinosaurs were understood to be an important group of animals, as each different dinosaur was discovered, it was given its own name. These names sometimes look very difficult to say and all of them come from Latin words. They usually describe something special about a particular dinosaur's appearance or habits – for example, Euoplocephalus means "well-armoured head".

How are fossils made?
A fossil is made when an animal dies and is buried in mud. Over a very long time the mud hardens and more mud is layered on top. Eventually it hardens into rock. Then, over millions of years, the rock is gradually worn away again, revealing fossilised bones.

How are dinosaurs reconstructed?

SOMETIMES SCIENTISTS FIND ONLY A FEW BONES, AND SOMETIMES THEY FIND WHOLE skeletons. Whatever the find, they always keep a careful record of how and where the bones were discovered. They take photographs and keep lists of everything. Then, when they have enough pieces of the puzzle, they are able to reconstruct whole dinosaurs or parts of dinosaurs and identify them. Scientists will often work together and can learn a great deal from the original notes made at dinosaur sites.

Palaeontologists work slowly and carefully, making detailed notes of their finds.

Who collected dinosaur bones?

People have been fascinated by dinosaurs and the science of palaeontology for over a hundred years. In Utah, in the USA, two men were largely responsible for one of the greatest dinosaur finds ever. They were Edward Cope and Othniel Marsh. In the Dinosaur National Monument, dozens of huge dinosaur bodies were found. In 1811 the first female palaeontologist, called Mary Anning, began work in Lyme Regis in England.

Edward Cope and Othniel Marsh made one of the greatest dinosaur finds in history.

What was palaeontology like 150 years ago?

The earliest palaeontologists simply collected the bones that they found or dug up, and tried to work out what they could be.

When a bone or part of a dinosaur turned up that had not been seen before, they would name it and try to work out what the animal must have looked like.

Gradually, over time, these early palaeontologists began to fit the pieces of the jigsaw together.

What is modern palaeontology like?

Modern palaeontology is much slower and more painstaking than it used to be. It is no longer simply a matter of collecting old fossils and bones. Modern palaeontologists take great care to preserve their finds and record them so that the information can be shared.

Everything we know about dinosaurs has come from more than 150 years of studying bones and fossils. Some palaeontologists have even gone back to old sites where bones have been found in the past, just in case the earlier scientists missed anything that a modern palaeontologist might find of value.

What is the future of palaeontology?

Thousands of dinosaur bones have been found and collected over the last 150 years. However, if the dinosaurs really did rule the world – and there were no other large animals in existence at that time – there must still be thousands of dinosaur bones that have not yet been discovered. There may even be hundreds of different kinds of dinosaurs that no one knows about.

The study of dinosaurs is likely to go on for a great many years to come, but in the end, maybe some of the big questions about them will be answered at last.

Index

Practical help fo
Decade o

CONTENTS

Enabling Church Planting

INTRODUCTION

Using this Book

What about copyright?

This material may be photocopied without charge for use in talks and discussion groups provided the © CPAS copyright notice is retained on each page.

CPAS places no formal restrictions on the number of copies made, but to permit the publication of further resource materials we recommend that each leader of a group purchases his or her own copy of this book.

This is the eighth in the series of CPAS evangelism resource books. These books are designed to be a practical resource for local churches. Although they are written mainly with Anglican churches in mind, we hope they will be useful to churches of other denominations too.

This book is intended as a tool-kit to help a church through the process of planting a new church. For those who simply want to learn more about the subject, it offers a good overview of the processes involved. But its principal aim is to provide planting teams and their leaders with resources and photocopiable material to generate discussion, aid decisions and bring the whole church along with the vision.

What's what?

The resource material falls into five sections, each with some or all of the following:

An *Introduction* page which outlines the contents of the section and features a real-life church plant story in five parts.

A *Briefing* paper on the theme of the section. This is either for a leader's own information or for photocopying and distribution to members of a planning group, church council or planting team.

One or more *Discussion* papers for group members. Again, these are designed for photocopying: they may not refer directly to the Briefing papers and so may be used on their own.

A collection of *Ideas* to provide starting points for further discussion and planning.

One or more *Illustrations* for talks or group work. They may contain cartoons or graphics. These illustrations may be photocopied on to acetate sheets for use with an overhead projector.

Is it a course?

Most of the materials in this book have been drawn from three regional *Planting for Growth* courses run by Anglican Church Planting Initiatives. They were attended by more than 200 people. Leaders may therefore choose to use it as a course for the planting team. Or they may prefer simply to use it for reference as they work through the process.

As the first chapter explains, this book is not a source of ready-made answers. Instead it offers practical, experience-based guidance for the whole of the church planting process.

Above all Get Understanding!

1

INTRO.

Contents

A three-page *Briefing* paper setting church planting within the current UK mission scene and introducing the planting process. Using both Old and New Testament, the authors examine the key biblical themes of mission, multiplication and incarnation.

A *Discussion* paper comparing the planting process to the human life cycle and containing a short Bible study on the parable of the farmer in Isaiah 28:23-29.

An *Ideas* sheet to help you think through how both the challenge and principles of mission affect you.

Extras

What is church planting?

Church planting is a broad concept covering a wide variety of creative mission projects. Here is how some have defined it:

'The transfer of part of a congregation into an area of need with the evangelistic expectation that new people will find faith and the renewal of their spiritual lives....' Archbishop George Carey

'Creating new communities of faith as part of the mission of God to express his Kingdom in every geographic and cultural context.' Bob Hopkins

In a phrase, church planting is *mission by forming faith communities*.

Spotlight on Cramlington: part one

Challenge to plant Cramlington is in Northumberland, some miles north of Newcastle-upon-Tyne. It was once a village, but has rapidly developed into a new town with a population of 35,000. Aware of the huge challenge facing them, the people of the parish church found themselves considering church planting as a way forward. Their story continues on each of the *Intro* pages.

Anglican Church Planting Initiatives

Churches and individuals interested or involved in church planting are invited to join this network. ACPI holds regular conferences and training events. We keep data on all Anglican church plants. We can put you in touch with other projects similar to yours. Individual consultancies are also available.

To join Anglican Church Planting Initiatives' free mailing list, please contact

ACPI
38 Lascelles Street
St Helens
Merseyside
WA9 1BA

Tel: (01744) 758886

For further information see **Resources** on page 40.

1 BRIEFING

Above all Get Understanding!

Well done, the fact that you are reading this means that you are taking the possibility of church planting seriously. A recent survey by one denomination showed that more than half of its church plants had gone ahead without their leaders having read a single book on the subject!

Many Anglican dioceses and deaneries are developing guidelines for church planting. These include policy on structural and financial issues and relationship to the wider church. Make sure you get all the help you can in this area.

The Urban Church Project

This project was commissioned by the General Synod of the Church of England in the mid Seventies. Contact Anglican Church Planting Initiatives for further information.

'I do not believe there is a biblical basis for mission! I believe mission is the basis of the Bible.'

Don Richardson

The mission field around us

Like it or not, the church in the UK and throughout the rest of Western Europe is in a classic missionary situation. In England, most people are no longer practising Christians. In the 1980s church attendance dropped by half a million people. Our society's values were once based on Christian principles. Now our diverse and rapidly changing culture offers a wide variety of competing value systems.

Throughout the nation there are neighbourhoods where there has been little contact with the church, in some cases for generations, and where the gospel has had minimal impact. This is equally true of many other social, cultural and ethnic groups. This has led some to challenge us to find new ways of 'being church'. In response, all the main denominations designated the 1990s a Decade of Evangelism.

Mission possible

Despite this overall decline, a quarter of all local churches in England grew by more than sixty-seven per cent during the years from 1979 to 1989. As well as finding effective means of reaching people, some of these churches planted new congregations. They met in secular buildings such as schools, community centres, pubs and clubs. Many of these church plants pioneered new models of leadership, new styles of worship and discovered a 'team dynamic' in their mission. This movement has grown across most denominations, with Anglicans planting some thirty-five churches each year since 1990.

Increase in Anglican church plants 1972–1993

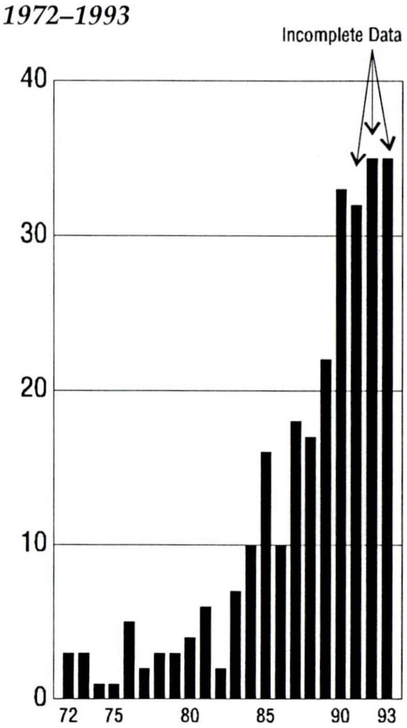

Church plants are happening in all sorts of social and geographical settings – urban, suburban and rural. In villages, the planting may be on a very small scale, or even be 're-planting'. In one Cumbrian community the small Methodist and Anglican congregations closed both their buildings and re-planted into a school. They described their project as 're-potting'.

Some church plants begin from a position of strength. They are initiated by large congregations and may have teams of more than twenty people. Others describe their experience as planting from weakness. They are prepared for the sacrifice of giving away a significant number of people even though there may only be between seventy and one hundred in the congregation.

From its work in many countries, the international movement called DAWN (Discipling A Whole Nation) has discovered that one of the most effective mission strategies is to work towards establishing one congregation to every 1000 people in the community. In England, this builds on a report published by the Urban Church Project. It showed that a single congregation is only most effective in reaching a parish population of not more than about 1800. Consequently, their second report used the challenging title *Towards the Multi-centred Parish*.

To make the most of this important movement in mission, we need to avoid competition or duplication and to plant in ways which do not threaten one another or cause division. There needs to be good communication, consultation and planning as well as new sorts of training for leaders and teams. Church planting is a very flexible and broad approach to mission offering many models from which to choose.

Is it biblical?

Here are three key biblical themes which shape our understanding of church planting.

1. *Mission* The whole Bible is a story of God's love reaching out to bring all of his creation into relationship. His main means of achieving this has been by choosing people to represent him, and to be his instrument to bring the rest of the world back to him. Jesus expressed this perfectly. He passed on a commission to his people (the church) to continue to make disciples from among every people group on earth – bringing them under the rule of his gracious Kingdom.

This means that the church's prime purpose and identity is found in the mission of God in the world. Archbishop William Temple said: 'The church is the only human society that exists for the benefits of its non-members.' Church planting focuses this mission in the faith community as it multiplies into every geographical and social context.

Bible focus

Read Genesis 12:1-5; Exodus 19:3-6; Matthew 28.

How much of your church's time, energy and money is directed outside itself?

How well do you think your people are gripped by this mission imperative?

2. *Multiplication* Jesus gave many parables of growth in the Kingdom of God. Matthew 13:33 expresses this in terms of almost limitless multiplication – a small amount of leaven can work through as much as twenty-two litres of dough! Jesus' words after his resurrection (Acts 1:8) promise that with the Holy Spirit's power his disciples will multiply as witnesses in an unstoppable wave from Jerusalem, Judea and Samaria to the ends of the earth!

Bible focus

Read Acts 1:8; 6:7; 12:24; 19:20.

The church's outward movement is emphasized in these three summary verses. It happened through two repeated phases – *increase* and *spread*. In the *increase* phase, centres of strength were established. There then followed dispersion, a *spreading*, with churches planted in every sort of place, beginning Christ's commission of a church among all peoples.

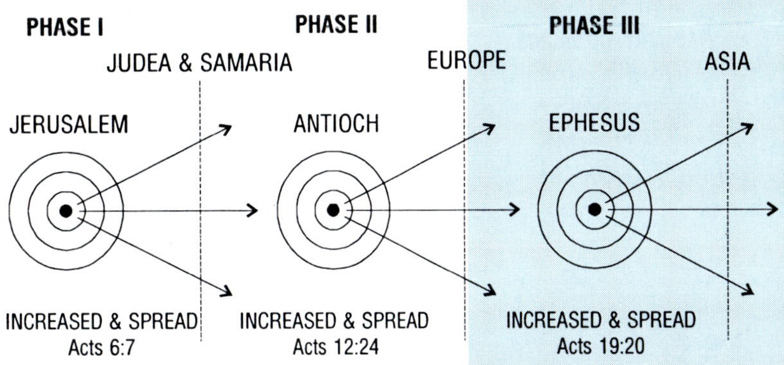

We could sum this up in an equation:

New Testament multiplication = increase + spread.

- Look at the story of the churches at Jerusalem, Antioch and Ephesus and find examples of the two phases of *increase* (concentration) and *spread* (church planting dispersion).
- How has your church been building up its human resources for mission?

BRIEFING 1

Above all Get Understanding!

'I have become all things to all men so that by all possible means I might save some'
1 Corinthians 9:22

'Church planting and similar radical mission initiatives are like the tug needed to help pull the liner of the whole church into mission mode.'
Robert Warren

3. *Incarnation* Jesus gave us a model of mission based on coming among us, being born as one of us. Paul spelt out similar principles underlying his church planting missionary journeys. He wrote of using 'all means to win some', becoming 'a Jew to win Jews and a Greek to win Greeks' (1 Corinthians 9:22).

Bible focus

Read Luke 10:29-37 (the parable of the Good Samaritan); Philippians 2:5-11; Acts 15:1-4, 19-21; 16:1-3.

Discuss how your church plant can express these principles and be an incarnation of the Body of Christ in new cultures and contexts.

Process

Have you ever felt frustrated after your church has tried a new evangelistic idea or programme? It should have had wonderfully fruitful results – but it didn't. The success stories you had read or heard about inspired faith that this one could be the answer. But they only increased the disappointment when the new plans failed. Why did a seemingly impressive package work so well in one context but show very little return in another, despite much effort?

Perhaps one answer is connected to our modern preoccupation with packages which offer instant results. We have become accustomed to supermarkets, to convenience foods and to microwave meals where following the instructions guarantees rapid success – or at least a refund.

However, advancing God's Kingdom is much more of a *process* than a *package*. It would be easy in this book to offer a ready-to-assemble DIY Church Plant Kit. But that would probably lead only to exhausted frustration.

Principles, people and prayer

Although no two church plants are identical, the process always contains three variables which constantly interact.

1. *Principles* Don't confuse principles with packaging. Ideas and programmes succeed because their underlying strategies are right. To distil the principles within a package, ask

- What was the strategy behind the approach?
- Why were those tactics appropriate to their situation?

2. *People* In every church and church planting team, a wonderfully unique group of people comes together as a missionary community. Their combination of personalities, gifts, experience, commitment and Christian maturity will affect every stage of the process as people and principles interact. They should develop a tailor-made evangelism strategy to serve the equally unique community of people they wish to reach.

3. *Prayer* God's people need to be open to his Holy Spirit's specific guidance through the process of applying general principles to particular situations. This is the most often neglected of the three elements.

Prayer track

'The army of God moves forward on its knees.' The best principles, enthusiastically applied, will achieve far less than their potential, if prayer is not seen as an integral part of the church planting process. For this reason each chapter's **Prayer track** will fuel ideas for prayer.

- Begin by praying that God will help you to see how the principles in this book affect the mission challenge faced by your own church.

Above all Get Understanding!

1 DISCUSSION

A life-cycle

The process of church planting has many similarities to human pregnancy. The life-cycle begins long before birth and continues long after it. Discuss as a team how the different stages of this process will be reflected in your situation.

Life-cycle of a reproducing church

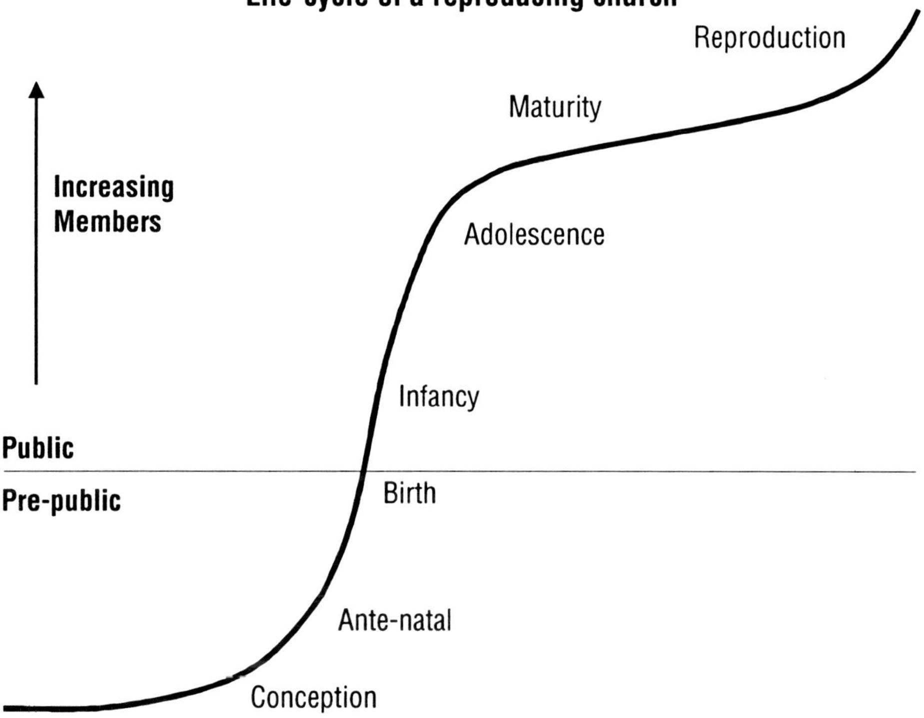

The parable of the farmer

Read Isaiah 28:23-29

This passage looks at a farmer involved in the physical 'planting process'. It includes a number of important pointers and keys for today's church planters.

1. Who is the farmer's teacher (28:26, 29)? Discuss how we should be guided in any planting process.

2. How does the farmer deal with different times (28:24), types (28:25) and textures (28:27,28)?

3. What does this teach about how God deals with complex and varied situations?

4. Make a list of guiding principles which would help you in the process of planning for planting.

Notes

Conception
Leaders and church members share a vision for outreach through a new community of believers.

Ante-natal
A team forms and begins research, outreach and prayer.

Birth
A new church is at last on public display.

Infancy
The young church learns to find its feet and may be dependent on its parent congregation.

Adolescence
The church becomes increasingly independent as it develops its own identity and ministries.

Maturity
It is ready to reproduce.

Above all Get Understanding!

Notes

Look again with missionary eyes

It's understandable for a thriving church with a large congregation to feel that it's doing very well. But the real challenge is to take a fresh look at the mission task and ask some difficult questions.

1. How well is your church doing in terms of its mission task?
   - What percentage of the parish's population attends church regularly?
   - Are attenders' homes spread evenly over your parish / mission area?
   - What explanation is there for any gaps or clusters in the pattern?

2. If every seat at each at your church's services was full
   - what percentage of the parish / mission area would be represented?
   - how many would still be outside the life of the church?

3. DAWN (Discipling A Whole Nation) offers strategy guidelines which suggest that to disciple an area effectively, there needs to be a witnessing community of believers meeting as church for every 1000 people in the population.
   - Assuming that's true, how many churches are needed to disciple your community / parish?
   - How do all of these questions affect the overall perception of how well your church is doing in mission?
   - What challenges do they raise?

Think *process* rather than *package*

Think of a couple of well-known 'packages' that are proving to be very effective tools in the life of some churches (for example, the Alpha Course).

- List the principles within those packages which may account for their success.
- Would changes need to be made to the way those principles are practised in order for them to be able to work well in your church and community?

The Seeds of the New Church

Contents

A two-page *Briefing* paper which outlines the importance of research in clarifying the initial vision for the plant, and which introduces different sizes of 'planting unit'.

Two *Discussion* pages looking at a variety of church plant models, and continuing to examine planting unit sizes.

A page of *Ideas* for helping the whole church unite around the vision.

A page of *Ideas* to help clarify the vision and develop a time scale.

A page of *Illustrations* which can be reproduced as OHP slides for use in sharing the church planting vision.

Extras

The planting process

Phase 1– conception

A healthy church plant begins with a clear vision. Just as at conception a baby's chromosomes establish its identity and much of its character, a strong original vision will influence and shape the new church's life as it develops.

Spotlight on Cramlington: part two

Twins on the way! Initial research into all six local denominations revealed a total church attendance of 1700 people. Comparison with census statistics showed this was five per cent of the population. The national average of attendance is ten per cent of the population. Furthermore, over 33,000 people were not in regular contact with any church. With a rapidly growing population, even increasing congregations represented a falling percentage of the total population.

Leaders in the Anglican and Methodist congregations investigated church planting as a mission response. For the Anglican church in particular, two areas provided obvious opportunities. Northburn, a new private estate on the edge of town, would be a 'progression plant' (for an explanation see page 13). On the other hand the much older development at Beacon Hill, although closer to the mother church, was largely untouched and would therefore be much more of a 'pioneer plant'. The two areas obviously needed different projects with different approaches.

St Nicholas, Cramlington, a very ordinary parish church of fewer than 200 members, had one extraordinary characteristic. Its people were prepared to take risks for such new life, even though in the previous decade an attempted plant into Beacon Hill had closed. Deciding to launch both church planting projects simultaneously, they resolved to learn from past mistakes and gave priority to careful planning and preparation. They also sought outside consultancy help and arranged for ongoing team training.

BRIEFING 2

The Seeds of the New Church

As the project develops, the vision will grow through two distinct phases. First it will be like a business 'feasibility study', defining the project's character, area, time-scale and potential leaders. The next phase takes the vision and develops it into a full church planting plan.

Vision – what is it?

Vision is the *shape* of things to come.

Vision is the *guiding* idea.

20:20 vision

Good vision both unites and motivates. As the church plant grows in numbers, and ages over time, a clear vision enables a group identity to be carried by all the members. Communicating the vision clearly and with conviction releases energy in the newly forming team.

To begin with, vision will depend on combining the facts uncovered by initial research with prayer. This is the church planting 'feasibility study'.

Initial research + prayer = initial vision

Write the vision

Initial vision will be much more useful if it is developed into a written statement. This should protect the church plant from those who may later seek to introduce their own personal vision. Obviously, writing the vision down doesn't mean it can never be altered. It simply ensures that if you do, you will know what you are changing.

For the written vision to be able to shape the new plant's character, it must be communicated again and again until everyone is deeply committed to it. *Say it, explain it and say it again.*

Initial research

Use a small task force to gain outline information very quickly. Some people have done this in one day. The aim is to come up with basic facts assessing both the need for a plant and its viability. (This is a separate task from the full Community Mission Audit outlined in Chapter 4.)

1. Buy two maps of the target area.
2. Select your target area or group through prayer and discussion. Mark it on your map. If the target group is a network of people, rather than a neighbourhood, consider their distribution across the map and discuss the best contact points to reach into.
3. Mark the homes of your existing church families on the map. Use the church address list or the local electoral roll. Alternatively, try putting a map and some pins at the back of church for several Sundays and ask folk to stick in pins to mark their homes.
4. Take a walk around the area. Pray as you go. On the second map mark significant details, such as all religious meeting places and any secular buildings which may possibly be used for the church plant.
5. Get basic details about the area from the Census. These will include population statistics with breakdowns of age, sex and cultural factors.
6. Now 'read' the community with 'mission eyes', discussing the key factors for and against different church planting possibilities.

'Write the revelation down and make it plain on tablets so that whoever reads it may run with it.'
Habakkuk 2:2

Planning – making it happen

It takes careful planning to make an exciting vision become a reality. As the planting process continues, you will need a full church plant plan. It should address the church plant's purpose, values, philosophy of ministry, style, priorities and programmes. The next chapter shows how further research is essential to the shaping of this plan. The skyscraper cartoon on page 16 illustrates how these elements fit together. ACPI produces a useful *Mission Statement and Planning Framework*: see **Resources** on page 40.

Different planting unit sizes

Although this book generally refers to planting teams, our observation is that there seem to be four different sizes of planting unit. Each size has its own characteristics and keys for success.

Individual / couple	1 or 2 adults
Small *team*	3 to 12 adults
Larger *group*	13 to 44 adults
Congregational *transplant*	45 or more

For cross-cultural projects, smaller units (individuals or teams) are most appropriate. Larger groups cannot easily adjust to a new culture, and tend to be rejected as 'incomers'.

The individual or couple *must* be gifted in evangelism and have a lot of perseverance. Of course, it also helps if they are multi-gifted!

Just as with the team, the larger group depends for its success on identifying and releasing the gifts of its members – especially the evangelists. The danger is that this need may not always be obvious to the members of the group.

Bible Society recommends that you shouldn't plant until you have fifty people. This doesn't refer to the size of the planting team, but rather the number at the 'birth'. They are happy for any of the above units to start the process, but recommend organic growth through evangelism to fifty people prior to going public. For a more detailed review of the issues of church plant size, contact the authors at ACPI.

Prayer track

The vision for a church plant is likely to be the result of combining facts with prayer. By seeing the present reality of the situation and, through prayer, having faith in what God wants it to become, a powerfully motivating vision is conceived. These very early days of the church planting process are a time of great vulnerability. It is wise to start praying as soon as possible.

- Plan an extended time of prayer: a day, half day or an evening.
- Identify those in the parent church who are intercessors. They may not necessarily be part of the new church plant, but can play a vital role in supporting it through their prayers. Recognize how valuable they are and encourage their involvement. Make sure you let them know about all answers to prayer.
- Prepare notes to help keep those praying in touch with the project and to highlight any needs.
- Fix a regular prayer meeting to intercede for the project, or make it the focus of an existing church prayer group.

Census information

The Government's Household Census is a source of very useful statistical information.

For help contact your public library, council offices or diocesan office. Alternatively, either Anglican Church Planting Initiatives or Challenge 2000 may be able to provide a census consultation for accessing computer data to produce maps and tables for a specified area.

DISCUSSION 2

The Seeds of the New Church

What sort of plant are you?

A few simple lessons from nature give some helpful insights into church planting. Plants reproduce in different ways. No two church plants begin in the same way. All the same, it's possible to do some helpful sorting into broad classifications.

Discuss how the following types of multiplication relate to planting a new community of faith. What are their advantages and disadvantages in different contexts? (See page 14 of *Church Planting: 1. Models for Mission in the Church of England*, Grove Evangelism Series 4, for a fuller development of these models.)

Runners

Some church plants may be like a strawberry runner, shooting off to form a daughter plant. The runner lasts for a while to feed the new plant. When it is well established the unneeded link to the parent will wither of its own accord. Plants formed in this way are genetically identical to the parent body.

A 'runner' church plant is usually established near to the parent church. It aims to reach people with a similar background to those who are already responding to the mother church's approach.

Seeds

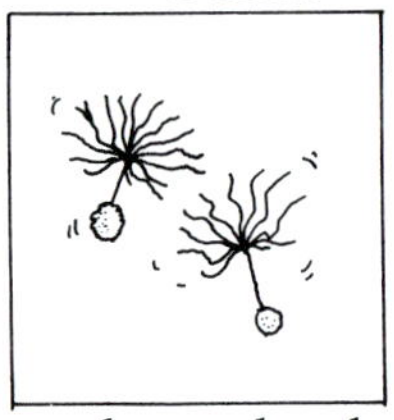

Some plants reproduce via wind-borne seeds. Although more likely to fail, the seeds can go further afield and are genetically different from the parent.

An example of a 'seed' church would be one established by a small team planting into an estate at the opposite end of a parish – or even further – from the main church. The aim is to reach people who are currently untouched by the ministry of the main church, and for whom its approach would not be relevant.

Transplants

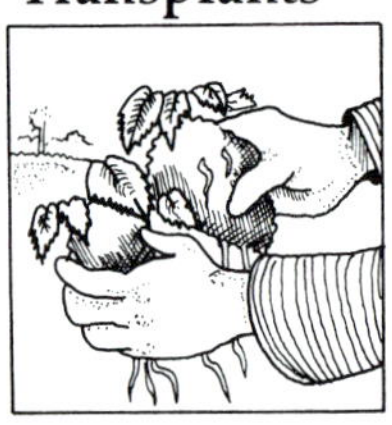

A gardeners knows how to divide a large plant into clumps and then transplant one part into a new place.

In some cases a large group moves out from a church and transplants a ready-made church. Some churches have sent out as many as between fifty and one hundred people to form a new congregation.

Grafts

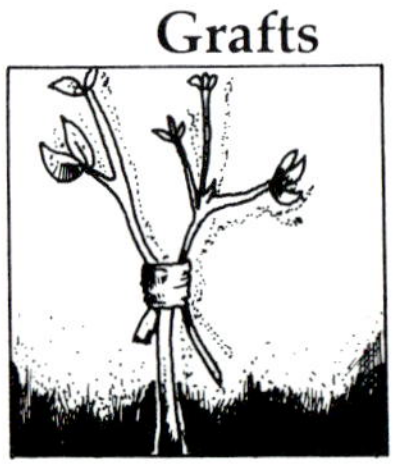

Sometimes a gardener grafts two plants together to obtain a special characteristic.

It is possible for groups to come together from two different churches to form a planting team. For example, a planting team may look for members from another church who are from the culture they are aiming to reach.

Further activity

In *Planting New Churches* (published by Eagle), George Carey and his fellow authors list seven types of planting (pages 16,17). These include multiple congregations sharing the same building, planting life into dormancy and planting into existing social structures such as clubs and homes for elderly people.

Review these and discuss which of them would be most applicable to your situation.

The Seeds of the New Church

2 DISCUSSION

Progression or pioneer?

Another helpful analysis of any church planting situation is to discover whether it is a progression plant or a pioneer plant.

Progression plants

Often the parent church already has members in the area or network which the church plant is aiming to reach. Forming a new congregation is not the first attempt to reach that community. It is part of a *progression* which focuses the life and witness of existing 'indigenous' church families. This mission strategy look for points of strength and builds on them.

Pioneer plants

When there are no Christians in the target area who have links with the parent church, then the planting team is beginning a completely new witness. This *pioneer* venture could well be inside the parent church's parish boundary – for example, on an estate so far untouched by the church. This mission strategy looks for areas of weakness and responds to them.

Crossing boundaries

Twenty per cent of all Anglican church plants cross parish boundaries and cause no problems because they are properly negotiated. Seed teams or grafts can work best in this kind of situation.

Discuss in your team which category your project falls into. (See pages 17-21 of *Church Planting: 1. Models for Mission in the Church of England*, Grove Evangelism Series 4, for more examples.)

Planting unit sizes

Review the descriptions of planting unit sizes on page 11.

Now discuss:

- What are the different dynamics of each unit?
- What are their advantages and disadvantages?
- What are the keys to making each one successful?
- Which unit size is your team likely to be?
- What principles should be kept in mind when working with that size of team?

IDEAS 2

The Seeds of the New Church

Unite around the vision

Any new project can threaten the unity of a church. All change challenges us and a church plant is one of the biggest changes a congregation will face. The following two exercises, when used alongside teaching and clear communication, have helped to transform opposition, reservations and mistrust into enthusiastic support. You may find doing them with the whole congregation one of the most important parts of the whole planting process.

Doubts and fears

1 Much opposition arises from misconceptions and from individuals feeling that their personal concerns are being ignored.

2 Reassure people that it's all right to disagree and to question things.

3 Split the congregation into groups of between five and eight members. Give each group some large sheets of paper and marker pens. Allow fifteen minutes for the groups to write down all their questions and doubts about the proposed church plant.

4 Stick all the sheets up on the wall. Give everyone time to see them over coffee or a lunch break.

5 After the break, review the lists and give honest answers. Allow time for explanation and discussion. It is helpful to suggest categorizing the questions into four groups:

- problems based on misunderstanding or miscommunication;
- problems which can be avoided or minimized by careful planning;
- those that are the unavoidable cost of mission and must be faced honestly;
- valid reasons to delay or cancel the church plant proposal.

The reviewer will usually be the person leading the exercise. In some cases you may want to invite an outside consultant to help. The process should happen with the whole group present and participating – in this way everyone can share in the difficult decisions regarding the realities of the 'unavoidable cost of mission'.

Best method

'Church planting is the best method of evangelism under God's Heaven', Dr C Peter Wagner, an acknowledged world expert on church growth.

Once their doubts have been aired, people are ready to listen to the positives and, best of all, to think through some for themselves.

1 Get people into 'buzz groups' of three or four. Put the quotation shown above on the OHP. Invite them to think why church planting may be so effective in evangelism. Ask them to consider why church planting may often be a more effective evangelism strategy than having one congregation simply growing larger and extending the building!

2 Once the groups have had several minutes to make lists, ask them to feed back their answers as you compile a master list at the front on OHP or flip chart. Make sure it includes comments such as

- 'Church planting puts evangelism at the top of the priority list.'
- 'It makes evangelism a way of life rather than a one-off event'
- 'It recognizes and values the gifts of evangelists in the team.'

The Seeds of the New Church

2

IDEAS

Design your own church plant

Sometimes it's good to dream big dreams. Think about how the church plant would be if you were completely free to choose every aspect of it. Be as radical as you like, but have reasons for all your choices.

Discuss each of the topics opposite and jot down how you would like to see your dream come true.

Try the same exercise with a neighbourhood or local social group and think through how effective your church would be in reaching those people.

- Building
- Worship styles
- Timing of services
- Midweek church life
- Outreach events
- Leadership structure
- Ecumenical stance
- Nurture programme
- Spirituality / tradition
- Social programmes
- Projected congregation size
- Baptism policy

Church planting planning chart	M1	M2	M3	M4	M5	M6	M7	M8	M9	M10
Research										
Initial project research										
Mission audit										
Leader and team										
Appoint task force										
Identify leader(s)										
Gather core										
Train core team										
Vision Development										
Write initial vision										
Develop strategic plan										
Share vision with PCC										
Share vision with church										
Share with wider church										
Prayer										
Arrange regular prayer										
Prepare prayer notes										
Prayer in area										

Planting a new church involves many overlapping tasks. Using a chart like this can provide an easy-to-refer-to picture of the main strands of the planting process.

God's creation shows the explosive power of multiplication

Where do churches come from mummy?

Leadership, Teams and Cells

Contents

A two-page *Briefing* paper explaining the importance of leadership, teams and cells in the early development of a church plant.

A *Discussion* page to help you review the sort of church you want to plant, and to help the team identify its shared area of agreement.

Three *Discussion* pages on leadership and team issues.

An *Ideas* page to help you develop your strategy for cell groups.

Extras

The planting process

Phase 2 – early pregnancy

A baby isn't born as just a set of chromosomes or a few cells. Every part is growing and developing long before birth. In the same way, the new church plant should go through a similar process of growing and developing its leadership, team life and structure before it 'goes public'.

Spotlight on Cramlington: part three

Team talk The two leaders of the Northburn church plant drew together a team of ten adults and eleven children. They believed that children were as much a part of the team as the adults. Consequently they planned a strong emphasis on children in the new church. The adults soon began team building. To help them they used games, 'gifting' questionnaires and organized social times.

Beacon Hill made a priority of identifying the very few Christians living on their estate. They formed a team around them. Here team building was just as important, but was far less structured in style. Tony, one of the leaders, noticed that the team found it difficult to pray aloud in meetings. He asked them to list things for which they were grateful and problems with which they needed God's help. They then turned those into short prayers. This simple exercise proved very effective in encouraging team prayer.

3 BRIEFING

Leadership, Teams and Cells

Leadership problems are the most common cause of weakness and failure in church planting. Church plant leaders should have a pioneer spirit, a heart for evangelism and perseverance. So the choice of those who are going to lead the new church must be undertaken with great care. Caution at this stage should prevent problems later on.

HEALTH WARNING

Church planting teams very occasionally cause unwanted side effects. Deep relationships formed can unexpectedly lead to inappropriate liaisons and even marriage breakdown. The authors can supply guidance notes.

Although most church plants have one overall leader, our Cramlington story is one of several examples of churches which successfully break this rule. The leadership team should have a 'breakthrough' quality – church planting is about bringing something out of nothing.

Different dioceses and denominations will, of course, have their own requirements for authorizing leaders and teams. What follows is guidance on general principles.

Leadership – what is it?

Management consultant Robert McLeish, a trainer with the BBC, teaches that leadership requires two qualities.

1. *Vision* This simply means knowing where you are going. It is crucial to know the final destination and the next step towards it. You don't, however, need to know *all* the steps to that destination. Moses knew he was leading God's people to a promised land, but he didn't by any means know all the stages along the way.
2. *Empowerment* Secondly, in the process of moving towards the vision, you need to 'empower' your people to get there. This involves team building, task setting, reviewing, resourcing, teaching, encouraging, training and praying. So much of what Jesus did empowered his followers. Leaders who do this make it possible for vision to be fulfilled even if, like Moses and Jesus, they are called away before arriving at the destination.

Leadership can be summarized in the equation:

Leadership = Vision + Empowerment.

It may be a surprise to see leadership pared down to only two elements. So often in churches, we expect many things of leaders which in fact should come under the heading of management and administration. As a result, instead of being 'future focused', they are dominated by here-and-now problems. They find themselves cornered into being busy, rather than effective. It can be very liberating for a leader to realize that he or she is not expected to be an expert in all areas of management and administration. If they were, there would be no point in having teams.

The River Church, Marlow

This growing church of more than 400 people has planted two congregations. But church leader Alistair Bullen does not work for it full-time. He says: 'I run my own design consultancy business to make as much money for the Kingdom as possible. How is it done? I recognized that over fifty per cent of what I would end up doing as a pastor would actually be administration. Most church leaders are not skilled administrators. It made sense to employ one. That's exactly what we did, and it seems to be working!'

Teams

Potentially the greatest resource for any church plant is a good team. The church planting process is a fantastic training ground for ministry. But sadly many churches often ignore vital principles which help make teams a blessing. If there aren't good relationships inside the team, potential blessing can become the curse of tension and division. The **Discussion** pages which follow develop key principles and give exercises to make the most of team life.

Cells

Once you have chosen a leader or leaders and formed a committed team, one of the next things to think about is cells or home groups. Study by church growth analysts has shown that healthy, growing churches usually function at three levels: cell, congregation and celebration.

Many churches have found that a structure of multiplying cell groups is the most appropriate for growth in the church planting process.

It is understandable for church planters to focus most of their energy on the Sunday meeting, the congregational level. It is all too easy to think: 'Yes, cells are a great idea. Once we have got established, then we'll need to think about them.'

Beware! You may well find that twelve months after starting, the demands of looking after the new church have increased. Simply trying to release people for roles within the church may be proving a frustrating impossibility. And as for cells? 'Oh yes, they're still a wonderful idea. We'll fit them in when we can!'

In the human body, by contrast, cells are the basic unit of growth. Many churches today are discovering that the cell is an essential aspect of being church. It is in small groups that new Christians can be nurtured, every member can actively participate and potential new leaders can be given the chance to learn by experience. It is only in small groups that people will feel safe enough to share their hearts openly and to build deep relationships.

Perhaps most importantly, the small group meeting is often the most effective place actively to encourage one another in personal evangelism. It can be much easier to have a 'seeker sensitive' small group to bring friends to, than to aim for the Sunday service to be their first non-threatening experience of church. It's not surprising that so much of New Testament church life revolved around meeting in homes.

Inspired by the unique effectiveness and biblical basis of small group meetings, some churches are becoming 'cell churches'. They still meet weekly for services or celebrations, but the cell has become the essence of what it means for them to be church. International church planting expert Ralph Neighbour predicts this movement will be 'the next reformation'! Even churches with more traditional structures see cells as a vital aspect of their life.

Cells are particularly important in church planting because they

- root the project in the community;
- centre the church plant around its organic life and most easily-multiplied unit;
- expand membership of the plant before public worship services begin, so that more people and resources are available for the public launch.

Prayer track

Prayer is the context in which leaders and teams hear God's call to the project. Perhaps the most effective activity for leaders seeking to empower their teams is to pray for them. It doesn't stop there, though. Every member of the team has a vital role to play in prayer as well as activity.

Build prayer into the routine life of leadership and team meetings.

Help your team sensitively over any hurdles they are struggling with regarding praying aloud during team meetings. (See *Spotlight on Cramlington* on page 17.)

DISCUSSION 3

Leadership, Teams and Cells

What sort of church to plant?

Many people have commented that whilst church planting in itself is an exciting mission strategy, it is vital that we are clear about what sort of church is being planted. Try the following two exercises as discussion starters.

1. What do you believe?

We all believe the same things, don't we? Possibly not. Some of us may think that certain doctrines are more important than others. Knowing how our 'Christian priorities' compare with those of the rest of the team can help to avoid painful conflict later on. Don't work on assumptions and then find out too late that you disagree on a fundamental issue!

- As a team, write a list of what you think are the twelve most important aspects of Christianity. The list opposite may help to get you started.
- Next, as individuals put them into order of priority.
- Now circle those which you think are 'truths necessary for salvation'.
- Discuss your results with one another. Now underline those items on which you will have to work together as a team to reach agreement – or simply agree to differ. Consider the implications of this exercise for the sort of church you want to plant.

◆ Conversion
◆ Divinity of Christ
◆ Baptism
◆ Creation
◆ Healing
◆ the Trinity
◆ the Church
◆ Salvation
◆ the Holy Spirit
◆ Holy Communion
◆ Sin
◆ Repentance
◆ the Devil
◆ Priesthood
◆ Resurrection
◆ Second Coming

2. Pictures of church

Rather than giving a systematic teaching on the church, the Bible is full of picture language which describes God's people, his church. In planting a new church, it is important to be inspired by what God intends the church to be. Try the following group Bible study for a fresh look at church.

Start by inviting everyone to close their eyes and make a mental note of the first image that enters their minds as you say each of the following words: church, bishop, saint. Explain that we all have 'subconscious' definitions based on our experience, even when we know that the Bible uses these words to mean very different things.

- As a group, brainstorm as many New Testament pictures of the church as possible (e.g. sheep, vine, body, bride....). Write them on a large sheet of paper.
- Add all the pictures you can think of from the Old Testament which describe God's people (e.g. nation, warriors....).
- Add major biblical themes which need to be taken on board in looking at the nature of the church (e.g. prophets, covenant, promised land....).
- Emphasize that the church is people, *not* buildings.
- Discuss how these pictures are shown (or not shown) in today's experience of church.
- Think through how you would like to see some of them made real in the church you are planting.

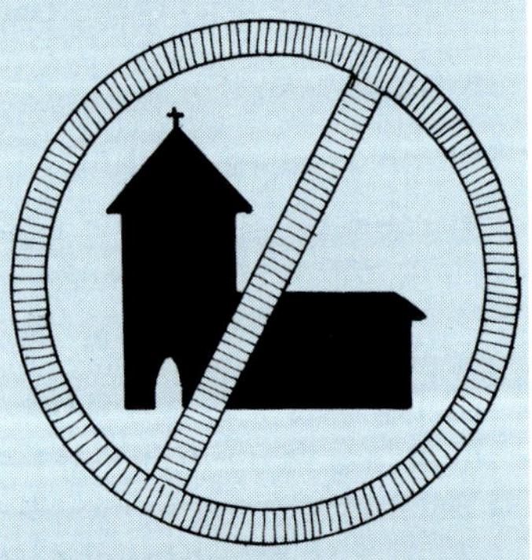

People not buildings

Leadership, Teams and Cells

3 DISCUSSION

Can you do it?

Notes

Focusing on what leaders do (*behaviour*) rather than on what they are (*qualities*) is a helpful strategy for potential leaders.

Work in small groups for this activity.

1. Make a list of the qualities of a good leader
2. Consider whether you now feel disqualified!
3. Now make a list of what a leader should *do*.
4. Does this feel more possible?
5. Finally list what Jesus did as a leader.
6. How does this compare with your lists?

Leaders, core team and others

As the leadership and the team develop, a three-fold structure usually emerges. First, there is the overall leader, or small leadership group of two or three.

They are supported by the core team, whose members are equally committed to the task. You need to rely on this team, so a basis of commitment should be agreed. For some this may involve serving for one or two years. Each core member should sense a clear call from God. This call should be tested by the leadership. The leaders may also, after prayer, invite people to consider joining. The core team is not for the first impulsive volunteers. The plant will not be served by motives such as: 'I never agreed with the vicar, or liked the services in the parish church.'

The third group will be people who want to join the plant once it has been launched, but for various reasons won't be in the core team through the planning stages.

- Using a larger version of this diagram, discuss the basis of commitment for your core team.
- Review and agree how you help people hear God's call, and how leaders reserve the right to test their call.
- Pray and begin to write in the names of possible team members.

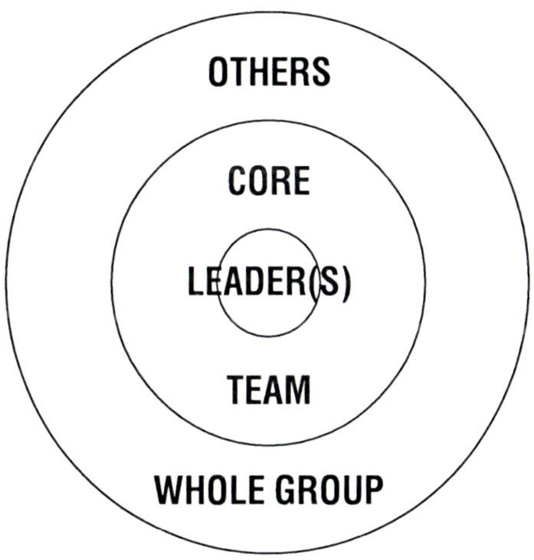

3 DISCUSSION

Leadership, Teams and Cells

Notes

Forming a team

'From him the whole body, joined and held together by every supporting ligament, grows and builds itself up in love, as each part does its work.' (Ephesians 4:16)

Work together as a team:

1. Paul links seven key verbs to the word 'body'. List them in the order in which they appear.
2. Consider this list as a description of the seven-stage process involved in forming a team, or in adding a new member to the team.
3. Decide what activities should feature in each stage of the process.
4. Note the importance of the order. We sometimes ignore the first six stages, assuming we should begin with 'work' – and then feel frustrated because the work isn't fruitful.

Think through how you can build these stages into your team formation.

Teams are complicated

A diagram of the relationships within many so-called teams would look like this:

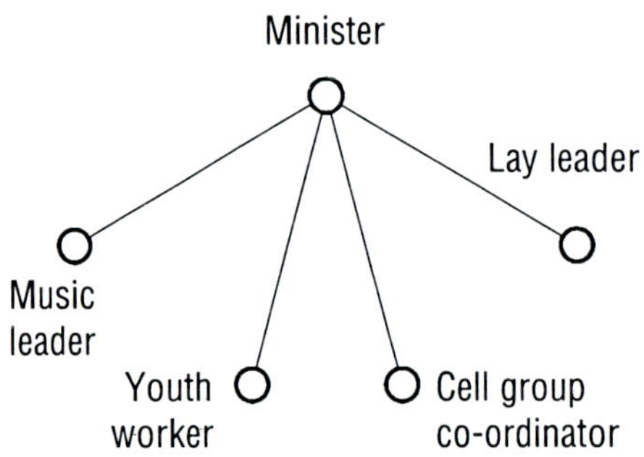

Four relationships

In fact this is not a team at all. It is simply a set of reporting relationships. It's like a football team in which players only ever pass the ball to their captain.

A good team is much more like this:

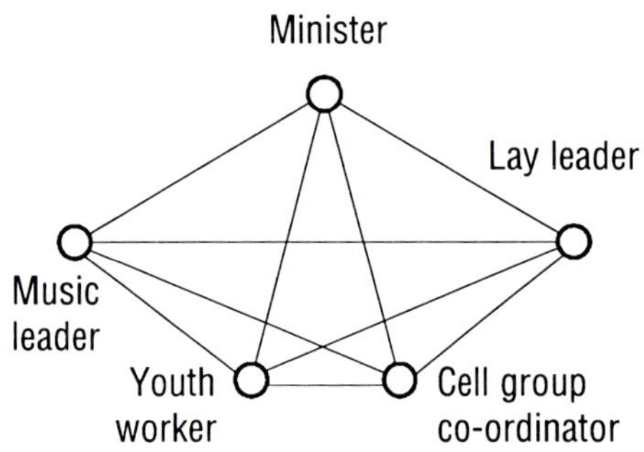

Ten relationships

This structure is much more complicated and requires more trust on the part of the leader because there are many aspects of team life which don't involve him or her at all!

As a team discuss which diagram most closely reflects your life together.

Ask each other: Are we really a team at all?

Draw your own team structure in the empty box opposite.

Leadership, Teams and Cells

DISCUSSION | 3

Good teams are all about differences

Members of effective teams can be thankful that any shortcomings they may have are probably balanced by the complementary strengths of others in the team. It is important to invest time and energy in understanding each other and the differences within the team. There are lots of useful tools to help in the process such as the CWR gift identification questionnaire, the Belbin team player roles and the Myers-Briggs or Enneagram personality tests. Used carefully as part of a well-prepared study of roles and expertise, these approaches can be a helpful addition to the team-building process.

Phase 1: dependent

Four phases of team life

Good teams go through four distinct phases. It can be liberating to realize that these are quite normal!

Most teams end at Phase 3. A lot of internal security is needed for going on to Phase 4. Fully inter-dependent teams are terrific, but the process of getting there is costly.

As a team discuss which stage you feel you are at and agree to review your progress through the church planting process.

Phase 2: counter-dependent

One Body, many parts.

Ephesians 4:1-16 presents an inspiring picture of different members in the Body working in unity. Sadly, we are often constrained by narrow interpretations of the ministry gifts in this passage. You may find the following descriptions expand narrow stereotypes and help in seeing how each person's gifts fit into the church planting team.

- Apostolic: pioneer, visionary leader, strategist, multi-gifted
- Prophetic: hear from God, know God's heart, worship leader, prayer motivator
- Evangelistic: proclaimer, people gatherer, inspirer to witness, enlightener
- Pastoral: carer, team / community builder, encourager, maintainer
- Teacher: explainer, trainer, exhorter, nurturer

Use these expanded categories to discuss team members' strengths. Try to identify any missing roles within the team.

Phase 3: independent

Phase 4: inter-dependent

Leadership, Teams and Cells

Notes

Cells

Do you have a carefully planned cell group strategy for the church plant?

How will you:

- equip cell leaders?
- monitor their progress?
- train new leaders?
- encourage every member to join a cell?
- see cells as central to the life of the church?

Keep reaching out

So often, home-based cell groups seem to end up as inwardly focused, pastoral meetings, making little use of their powerful potential for outreach. Through wanting to develop deeper fellowship, Christians often resist their cell's evangelistic possibilities. Discuss how you can make sure this doesn't happen. Some ideas others have used include:

1. Encourage cells to go *up* (prayer and worship), *in* (fellowship and learning) and *out* (evangelism projects).
2. Have joint leadership in each cell with a 'pastor' and an 'evangelist' complementing each other.
3. End every meeting with a 'share the vision' time of prayer for non-Christian friends.
4. Make regular times in the cell to encourage each other in the process of building friendships outside the Christian community.
5. Set a 'D Day' (say twelve to eighteen months after beginning) by which each cell aims to multiply itself.
6. Don't feel you have to do all of the activities every time you meet.
7. Stay fresh! Plan your programme as a series of seasons. Include breaks, have social activities and make time for training in specific areas.

Rehearsal for understudies

Base cell reproduction on each leader within the cell (the nucleus) training an understudy. These roles may include: host, worship leader, pastoral leader, outreach leader, a 'catalyst' (someone who gets people mixing) and prayer motivator.

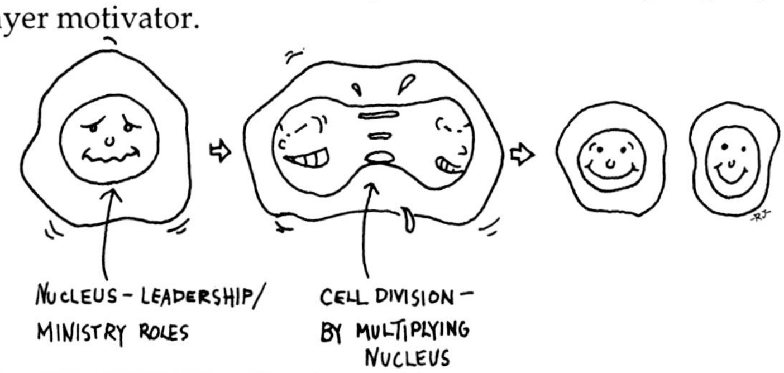

Developing Outreach Strategies

4

INTRO.

Contents

A four-page *Briefing* looking first at the importance of research in the church planting process and emphasizing the importance of the Community Mission Audit. The second part describes a framework to help plan for outreach to different groups in the community.

An *Ideas* page with suggestions for developing confidence in personal evangelism.

A *Discussion* page with exercises to help the team develop evangelism strategies.

An *Ideas* page to support the Community Mission Audit.

Extras

The planting process

Phase 3 – later pregnancy

The church's leadership and team structures should be developing in the pre-birth months. At the same time strategies for outreach should be set in motion. Church planting can be an opportunity for those who have loathed traditional approaches to evangelism to discover new ways of reaching the community.

Spotlight on Cramlington – part four

Homework Northburn's team leader happened to be a statistician. His analysis of the information provided by their survey helped form an outreach strategy with several 'sowing strands'. Most residents had moved into the area in the previous five years. They shared a lack of sense of community and a fear of burglary. The planting team produced a good quality neighbourhood newspaper. They encouraged residents to support a neighbourhood watch scheme. They also organized a car treasure hunt that attracted eighty people. As part of it they pitched a marquee at the entrance to the estate with displays and opportunities for tea and chat. Their children's sports day was also a great success, with invitations delivered to houses where the community survey had shown there were children of the appropriate age.

The church plant at Beacon Hill took a different approach to 'doing their homework'. Their response to their research was different, too, so as to fit their different social context. On housing estates, surveys can raise suspicions of 'the Social' checking up. They used contacts who were already known in the neighbourhood. They realized that although relatively poor, folk on Beacon Hill were very generous. With this in mind the church planting team helped people on the estate respond to the needs of orphans in Romania with clothes collections, bring-and-buy sales and other fund-raising efforts.

4

BRIEFING

Developing Outreach Strategies

Most church planting teams try to carry out a thorough Community Mission Audit in preparation for the launch of the new congregation. This is much more than an information-gathering exercise. To see it as such is to risk a tragic lost opportunity. The audit can be the vitally important first phase of the mission – it's the best way to start your outreach.

> *'We invite every Baptist congregation in the world to establish, or to explore the possibility of joining with other churches in establishing at least one new congregation by 2000 AD.'*
>
> **The Derbyshire Declaration, adopted by the World-wide Baptist Movement**

Doing your homework

Do you know the facts? It seems incredible, but so often Christians put a lot of time, energy and money into programmes without ever engaging in what the business world calls market research.

The apostle Paul spent time researching the ways of life, types of people, worship practices and even local literature of an area before he began to plant a church. He recognized the foolishness of investing so much effort in mission without doing his homework. In the Old Testament great leaders such as Moses, Gideon and Nehemiah realized that it wasn't unspiritual to find out the facts before moving towards a promised land, conquering an enemy or building a city wall.

As you work through the church planting process and plan a clear outreach strategy, it is essential to know the facts. There are three main ways of discovering these facts:

- *Observation* Walking around the area, praying and making notes.
- *Conversation* Talking to key people at length about the area. Then doing a much wider survey covering a good proportion of those you are seeking to reach.
- *Investigation* Unearthing vital information about the social, economic, historical and spiritual state of the area.

In each of these fact-finding methods, there are three types of information to look for:

- *Physical* Houses, buildings, amenities, roads.
- *Social* Community needs, recreational and commercial facilities, employment, people's perceptions of the community.
- *Spiritual* Factors that have influenced the spiritual state of the people you are aiming to reach.

Make the most of it

As you plan how the team can be involved in this process, it is important to realize that there are three important aspects to the survey work.

1. The information itself will be extremely valuable to help planning.
2. The work of surveying the neighbourhood, meeting and interviewing local people, will affect the team. It's the best preparation for the mission of the church plant, giving them understanding of the local context and of God's heart for the people and the area.
3. If it's done with prayer and faith, the survey and visiting can lead to key contacts in the community. When Jesus sent his disciples ahead, he told them to expect 'men of peace' to welcome them and to be the entry point into networks in the community. If we respond to people sensitively, it sets a positive image of the new church in the neighbourhood.

Members of a church plant in Manchester were praying as they did their neighbourhood survey. One of the team felt God directing her to go to a

particular house in Forest Road. Nervously she visited that house and found that the mother had been looking for a church to go to. Following this meeting, the whole family came to Christ and became the church's key link into the community!

Evangelism that works

Peter Wagner's belief that 'Church planting is the best method of evangelism under God's heaven' underlines the fact that reaching new people is the whole aim of a church plant. Many, however, don't realize that the ideal time to start this is well before launching public worship. If you wait until then, the team may get so swamped with all the new tasks of running a Sunday event in a hired building, that there's little time left for outreach. If evangelism is to be the top priority, it needs to become a way of life from early on. Ideally, it flows from the neighbourhood survey work in the ante-natal phase.

Is evangelism the one activity you secretly love to hate? Have you been disappointed through previous efforts at evangelism? Certainly it must be one of the most talked about and least practised parts of church life. It need not be so.

Laurence Singlehurst, the English director of Youth with a Mission believes that most Christians, when asked, admit to disappointment in their experience of evangelism. In his book *Sowing, Reaping and Keeping – people-sensitive evangelism* he claims that 'you need never be disappointed again!' This Briefing draws extensively on the fresh approach he has helped many churches to take in evangelism. Because his approach gives a structure suitable for developing in any neighbourhood or community, it is ideal for use in church planting.

Event or process?

Laurence asks people for their definition of evangelism. Common answers include: communicating the Christian faith; a lifestyle that shows Jesus to others; explaining the gospel to others...and so on. 'Why were you disappointed in past evangelistic efforts?' he goes on to ask.

The usual replies are: 'Very few people became Christians'; 'No-one responded'; 'It simply didn't work.'

Laurence comes back: 'So you describe evangelism as a *process*, but subconsciously believe it to be an *event* – the event of leading someone to Christ.' This is an attitude which we must unlearn.

The evangelism process

The Engel Scale

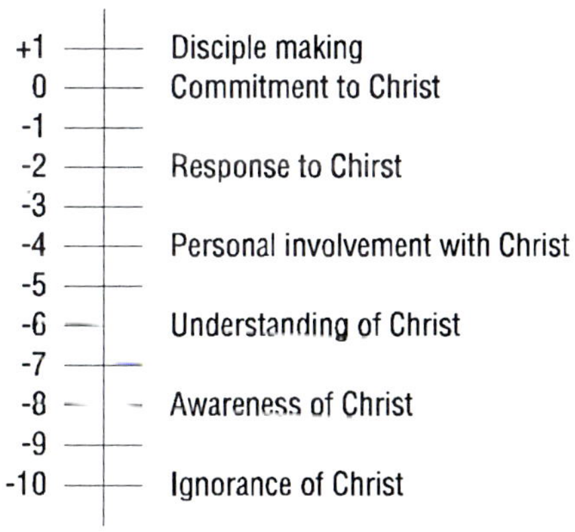

The process of evangelism can be shown using the Engel Scale.

Evangelism is simply about finding folk at whatever point they are on the scale, and influencing them on their journey towards faith in Christ. Moving someone from -10 to -8 is just as much evangelism as moving someone from -2 to 0, the point of conversion.

Evangelism is not leading people to Christ! Instead, leading people to Christ is *one part* of evangelism. So be careful about how you celebrate when someone does lead a friend to Christ.

Prayer track

'And pray for us, too, that God may open a door for our message, so that we may proclaim the mystery of Christ....' (Colossians 4:3)

Evangelism without prayer has been described as an explosive without a detonator.

- As a team, share your fears and past disappointments in evangelism. Pray for each other, especially for the ability to be an effective witness among non-Christian friends.
- Mobilize prayer support for specific outreach plans as they are decided and implemented.
- Pray for non-Christian contacts made during community survey and outreach events.
- In your prayer, be open to God giving impressions which will shape or direct your outreach.

4 BRIEFING

Developing Outreach Strategies

> *Do you not say, 'Four months more and then the harvest'? I tell you, open your eyes and look at the fields! They are ripe for harvest. Even now the reaper draws his wages, even now he harvests the crop for eternal life, so that the sower and the reaper may be glad together. Thus the saying 'One sows and another reaps' is true. I sent you to reap what you have not worked for. Others have done the hard work, and you have reaped the benefits of their labour.'*
>
> **(John 4:35-38)**

For help and encouragement on making the most of opportunities presented by Parent and Toddler Groups, see *Reaching Young Families* by Judith Wigley, published by CPAS.

It's easy to communicate an unspoken message that he or she is now a *real* evangelist, thus devaluing everyone else's hard work in the process.

Sowing and reaping

The fourth chapter of John's Gospel gives the account of Jesus meeting the Samaritan woman at the well. He explained (John 4:35-38) to his disciples that evangelism is a process of *sowing* and *reaping*. Yet so often in our evangelism we've ignored the sowing and become totally focused on reaping. We expect people to respond and make a life commitment on their first encounter with the gospel. The only time we usually talk of sowing is when we have presented the gospel with a challenge to respond, and no one does. 'Oh well, seeds were sown,' we console ourselves when probably people were put off by ill-timed reaping.

When Jesus spoke to the Samaritan woman, he recognized from her questions that she had a great deal of knowledge about God and the scriptures. In other words, she was quite a long way up the Engel Scale. He pointed out that others had done the harder work of *sowing*, so that he was able to *reap*.

Imagine by contrast, standing on your high street and asking people what they thought of God. They might describe an old man unmoved by human suffering, or perhaps a vague universal force. What if you then asked their opinions of Christians and the church? The enthusiastic response is likely to be: 'Boring weird hypocrites.' Expecting someone in that state to make a commitment is the same as asking him or her to believe in a monster and join the most boring group of people on earth. No wonder we become disappointed!

Many of the unchurched people whom we meet are very near the beginning of the Engel Scale. They need to make a journey of discovery about Christians and their God before they are in a position to make a lasting, heartfelt commitment to Christ and his church.

So what is sowing in our culture? Laurence contends that it's simply helping people discover that 'God is good and we're OK!' There may then be an opening to communicate slowly the meaning of the gospel. Gradually they will begin to open up to the gospel message and how it works in our lives. Only as they reach that point should we dare to confront them with a decision.

In *Finding Faith Today*, John Finney's research shows that in an overwhelming number of cases, it's relationships that support and draw people through the faith-finding process. Laurence Singlehurst shows how relationships and social contacts can be most effectively developed to reach different groups.

You need a strategy

The Parent and Toddler Group has been going for several months. Twenty-five non-Christian adults have been attending regularly, and a few seem to be getting interested in finding out more about Christianity. The best idea seems to be to bring in an 'evangelist' at Christmas time to give a ten-minute talk, to which the adults can 'make a response'. Sadly though, they do not receive the talk with much enthusiasm. The following week only ten turn up. The rest left because they felt violated. They had chosen to come to a Parent and Toddler Group, not a Christian gospel meeting. The goal posts had been moved.

So what's the answer? Obviously individual Christian helpers at the group carried on with personal evangelism. But the group can have much greater evangelistic potential than that.

Switching to another analogy, Laurence suggests thinking of our strategies as a succession of pools. These pools progress from cold, to warm, to hot. The problem with the Parent and Toddler Group was that its leaders turned up the heat and most of the fish jumped out.

The answer is instead for our 'cold pool' Parent and Toddler Group to stay as it was, a much-appreciated, high-quality service to local families. But linked to it, the church opened up a channel to a series of other pools, each warmer than the last. In this way, those who are ready for something warmer *choose* at their own pace to move on to the next pool.

An effective strategy will have at least five stages:

1. *Sowing one* A social event to meet a felt need and build relationships. Contact between Christians and non-Christians will begin the process of discovering that 'God is good and we're OK'. For unchurched people, for example, the Parent and Toddler Group would be the perfect venue as it has no gospel content at all, except when Christian people give answers to direct questions.
2. *Sowing two* A further social gathering, but more overtly Christian with occasional talks on faith related to life issues. An example of this for our parents would be to advertise a monthly coffee morning, where they can grow in friendship. The Christian parents would feel more free to share their faith. Occasionally there could be an advertised speaker – for example, a visiting parent sharing how her faith helped her through the 'terrible twos'!
3. *Sowing three* A context in which the essentials of the gospel can be presented in a natural way, over a period of time. For the parents, this could be a regular pram service (possibly arranged to fit in with school pick-up times) where aspects of the Christian faith are explained, but with no challenge to take a decision, other than the possibility of joining an enquirers' group.
4. *Reaping* A special evangelistic opportunity to hear the gospel and make a response. For example, there could be invitations given at the pram service to attend an evangelistic meeting for parents. These would clearly state that the gospel will be presented with opportunity to respond.
5. *Keeping* must be the next stage – to nurture those who do respond.

Reaching new groups

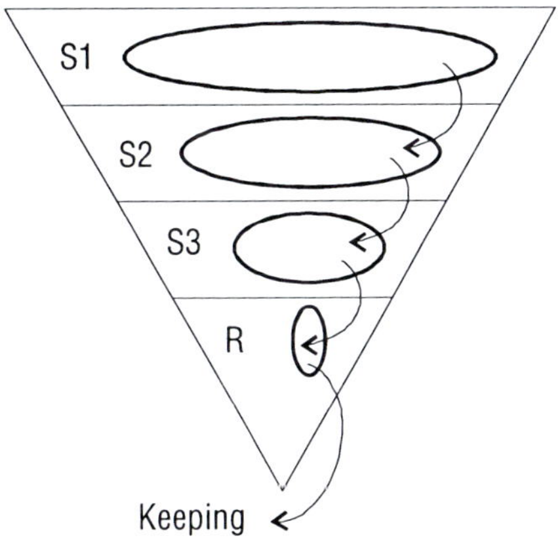

This shows the principles behind our strategy for reaching a new group. At the top is the biggest number of people, but the smallest gospel content. At the the bottom of the triangle are the fewest people, but the largest gospel content.

> ***'Increasingly we need to see the "doing" of evangelism as the creation of frameworks within which people can discover the gospel at their own pace.'***
> **Gavin Reid**

Summary of the strategy principles

- It is a process with several distinct phases.
- At the sowing end of the process, there is the largest number of people and least gospel content. The reaping stage has the fewest people but the largest gospel content.
- There is a channel from each pool to the next.
- People *choose for themselves* if and when to go through the channel and move on to the next pool.
- There are realistic expectations of what each phase is meant to achieve.

4 IDEAS

Developing Outreach Strategies

For help and encouragement on how to share your faith, see the first evangelism workbook in this series: *Creating Confidence in Evangelism*, by John Young.

The Alpha course

- If your group does not already know about the highly successful Alpha courses currently being run by many churches in the UK, make it a project to research them and discuss their suitability to your church plant. You may also want to look at resources such as CPAS's *Christian Basics*.
- Lead a discussion in your church planting team on where you think the Alpha course fits into the triangle strategies of Sowing, Reaping and Keeping.
- Consider how your church plant would generate contacts eager to come to a first meeting of an Alpha course.

In our view, the Alpha course is a brilliant evangelistic tool because it covers all the steps of our strategy from the second stage of Sowing to the last one of Keeping. Many forget how important it is either to have a really good idea for the first stage of Sowing, or to have a strong background of well-mobilized friendship evangelism.

Tell your friends

As well as the above planned outreach strategies to reach particular groups in the church plant's target community, your team needs to be inspired and helped to reach their network of relationships. There are many materials and courses available to encourage personal evangelism.

- Appoint a team member to research these resources, and hold a team meeting to decide which you will use as a team – and also for training new folk drawn into the church plant.
- Get each team member to write out his or her testimony / faith story. Share them in pairs, listening out for any Christian jargon.
- Do team role plays of how you would share the heart of the gospel message with an enquirer who was very open to it.

Try a field trip visit!

One of the best exercises is for leaders and team to visit an established church plant which has the benefit of two or three years' practical experience. ACPI can help link you to a church plant which is broadly similar to your own.

Developing Outreach Strategies

4 DISCUSSION

What's your strategy?

1. Men in the pub

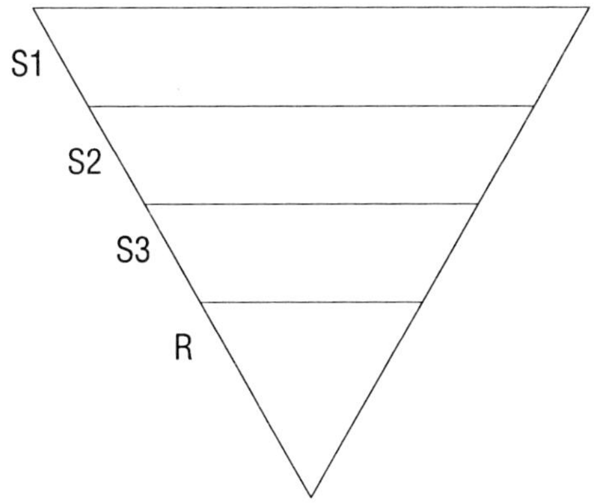

2. Unchurched youth

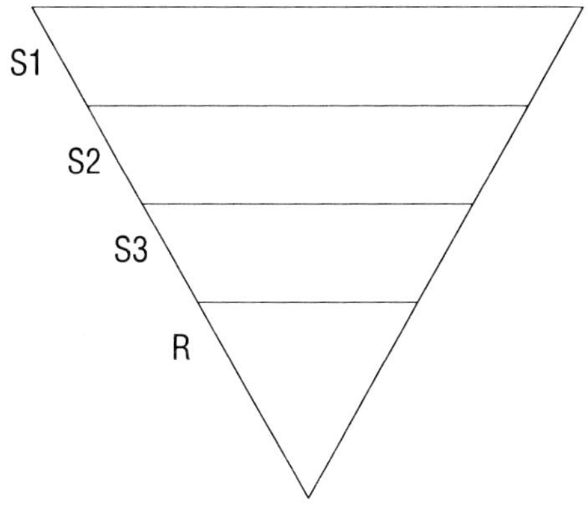

3. Retired people

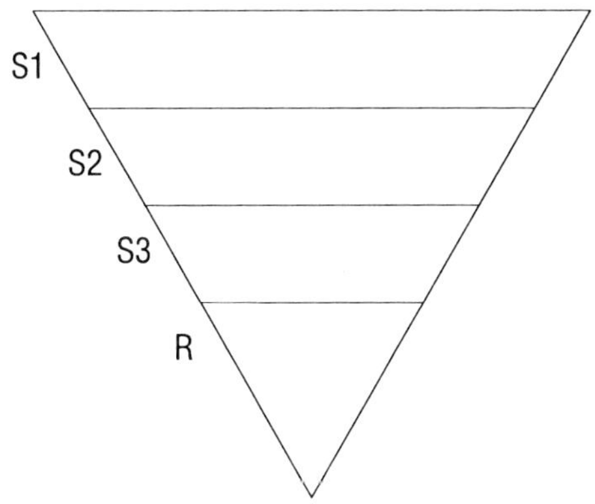

4. Your choice

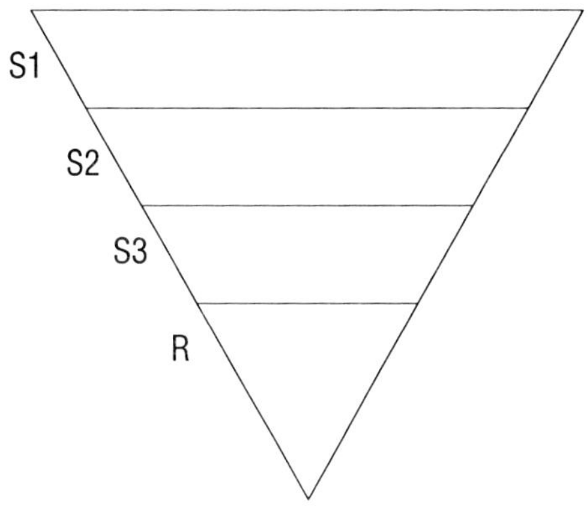

1 If possible, copy each of these triangles onto a large sheet of paper.

Taking each of the first three triangles in turn, brainstorm your own ideas of appropriate 'cold' to 'hot' pools to help members of each 'people group' move forward on their faith journey.

For the fourth triangle, choose a specific group which you have identified as being important in your church planting context.

2 Developing an evangelism strategy should not mean starting a lot of completely new activities. Instead the process should involve looking at where all the church's current activities fit in, identifying gaps and adopting appropriate expectations for each activity. It is also an ideal exercise to stimulate evangelism in an existing church.

- Take another large sheet of paper and draw one very large triangle like those in the previous exercise. *Around* the triangle write all the activities that your team already undertakes (individually or as a group) which bring you into contact with people outside the church family.
- Next, write these activities into the appropriate sections *within* the strategy triangle.
- Now pick a people group in your area, and see which existing activities already relate to them, and what other activities you would need to complete a strategy for them.
- Discuss how individuals in each group would go through the evangelism process. If it seems worth following up, write out a separate strategy triangle for this people group.

4

IDEAS

Developing Outreach Strategies

Notes

How to do your homework

Interviews Talk to two long term-residents of your target area about its history. Talk to two people whose work in key jobs in your target area gives them access to the community – shop-keepers, health visitors, community centre staff. Ask them what opinions people express about the community.

Survey First decide on how much information and interaction you are aiming for in your community assessment, then begin to plan your neighbourhood survey.

Choose the questionnaire There are several excellent neighbourhood questionnaire forms available, such as the one in *Creating a Church for the Unchurched* by Anne Hibbert. Discuss which best suits your needs, or whether you need to write your own. The questionnaire must be one which the team feels confident using.

Determine the sample In the light of the size of population in your target community, and the human resources and time available to the team, decide whether you will survey every house, or only a proportion of them.

Involve the team Talk about any fears about 'door knocking'. Dispel any myths about needing to be confrontational.

Inform the community Consider leafleting the community you will be surveying, explaining that you will be visiting with a questionnaire as you are planning a new project and need their opinions. This small step of politeness may entirely change the way you are received.

Get out there After praying, go out as a team to do the questionnaire. You may want to split up and go at different times to find different sections of the population at home. Be sensitive to elderly and lone residents who shouldn't be encouraged to invite strangers into their homes.

Draw conclusions Choose a member of the team who can analyse all the completed questionnaires and prepare a summary from them.

Plan and give feedback Find out if people in the community would like to know the results of the survey. Arrange to make follow-up visits as appropriate, or arrange a display in a local public building.

Books and archives Visit your local library and council offices to obtain historical and socio-economic information on the target area.

The Census A wealth of statistical information is available from the Government's 1991 Household Census. This can be accessed from public libraries, council planning offices or diocesan offices. Alternatively, either Anglican Church Planting Initiatives or Challenge 2000 may be able to provide a census consultation for accessing computer data to produce maps and tables for a specified area.

Birth and Beyond

Contents

A three-page *Briefing* highlighting the key stages in the birth and early life of the new church.

A *Discussion* page to help plan for the discipleship and nurture of new members.

Two pages of *Ideas* on issues of worship and growth in the new church.

Extras

The planting process

Phase 4 – birth and beyond

Many people have commented that the biggest change a couple will ever live through is the arrival of their first child. In the church planting life-cycle, the time when the church goes public is equivalent to birth. The community becomes fully aware of the new congregation. In many cases this will coincide with the first public worship service. A birth calls for great celebrations. You only have one chance to do this, so plan and prepare carefully to make the most of all opportunities.

Spotlight on Cramlington: part five

Launch Day After more than a year of planning, preparation and outreach, the two new churches were launched in the same month. On 3 October 1993, St Peter's, Northburn held their first public worship service with a total attendance of 148, of whom ninety-nine were complete newcomers.

Two weeks later, and prepared for a much smaller response, St Andrew's, Beacon Hill, was born. Again the numbers attending proved that all the thorough preparation was well worth it. Of the seventy-two at the first service, only ten were members of the planting team. Bearing in mind their target community, this was perhaps an even more dramatic result than Northburn's.

Average attendance figures have now settled down to eighty-five for St Peter's and sixty for St Andrew's.

Such effective outreach creates plenty of needs. The infancy stage surprised both teams with its busy-ness and stresses. They had to find ways of releasing new people to tackle necessary jobs. But much like the red-eyed parents of newborn babies, the people of Cramlington wouldn't trade their twins for anything else.

The Cramlington story is available on video – see **Resources** on page 40.

5 | BRIEFING

Birth and Beyond

Church planting has a great advantage. It makes it possible to start from scratch. Most leaders would give their eye teeth for this unique opportunity to set properly in place every part of the church's life. It's a chance that doesn't come often. Make the most of it!

> ***'Planting new congregations enables churches to reach out with a locally accessible centre of Christian worship, witness and service.'***
> **Bishop Patrick Harris**

Birth – the details

Birth Couples having their first child are invariably surprised at the amount of equipment to get and details to arrange. Most would say that the arrival is the biggest change they ever experience. The launch of a church plant is no different.

Buildings Although the building is the first thing most people involved will think about, there are other much more important aspects of the church plant – the people who will meet in it, their worship and life together. Nonetheless, it's important to choose your building carefully. Points to look for include:

- Central and convenient location for the target neighbourhood or network – perhaps an already known community venue.
- Plenty of parking space – but beware of upsetting the neighbours.
- Suitable size of meeting hall – big enough for growth, but not so big that people feel lost in it. If this is a problem, you may be able to partition a large hall until the church plant grows.
- Facilities for any children's work.
- Storage space for equipment.
- Easy access. Will you depend on a friendly caretaker?

Resources for the building and worship services List all that will be needed: chairs, PA system, table for Communion, overhead projector, song books and so on. If the church plant is to meet in a hired building, plan how you are going to create an atmosphere of worship and minimize distractions. Does the building need to be licensed?

Finalize the initial ministries of the new church The different task groups should be ready to take up their roles in the new church. It can be quite a shock after the build-up to the first public worship service, to realize that this one is only the first. There will also be one next week, and the week after, and the week after that – no let-up! The task groups should therefore have worked through details of planning worship services and other aspects of church life, including:

- Leaders and teachers. Who are they? Will you have teaching themes?
- Practical jobs. Are there teams to set up and clear away the chairs, to make coffee...?
- Teams to welcome people at the door. Do they know how to be friendly without being threatening?
- Children's programmes. Will there be all-age worship, or children's groups?
- Pastoral care and visiting. What is the church's pastoral strategy? What follow-up will there be for new arrivals?
- Communion Services. Who will preside? How frequently will they be scheduled?

These are all in addition to the ongoing ministries of the cell groups and of outreach.

Music It's vitally important to know which styles of music are most appropriate for the church plant's community. Don't rely on personal preferences. The music group and its leader should have been preparing since long before the launch. Build worship into the life of the team so that at the first public service, its members will

be used to worshipping together and can give a lead to everyone else. If you are using OHP transparencies for songs, check whether or not you will need a copyright licence.

Have a dry run Many church plants have found it invaluable to have a 'dry run' service with only the team present. In doing so, many of the 'bugs' will become obvious and can be fixed before the public service. Take time to pray together in the building about its use. Whatever the venue, it's important that it should be a place of prayer.

Team commissioning and 'send-off' The launch will be a time of bereavement for those in both the mother church and church planting team. All the same it's important to make a really positive focus of sending off your missionary group at a special service. The Bishop or another representative of the wider church may want to come and pray for the team and the 'sending church' as both face the new mission challenges.

Celebrate the birth Make the most of publicizing the birth of the new church. Most communities are very surprised when they see a church doing something new, so re-visit any positive contacts from your survey work. Consider leafleting the area. Contact local newspapers and radio stations.

Transition – from planting team to new church One of the most important things to prepare for at birth is a change in the thinking and identity of the members of the team. This is often forgotten or not understood.

A planting team should be a tightly-knit group with a clear basis of membership and a firm commitment to a shared goal. The planting task will take a very high priority in the lives of the members of the core group. From the day of the launch, however, this close circle must open up to welcome others. The primary aim of the new church is to draw others in – and not as spectators. The primary focus should now be much more on the well-being of the new church.

New arrivals will have all sorts of different understandings of the church and of the Christian faith. They must not feel like outsiders with the team appearing to be the in-crowd. The art of church planting is to lose the exclusive ethos of the team at birth, but to maintain all its advantages of motivation, energy and effectiveness! Consider how you can best achieve this in your situation.

Growing up

Infancy – a messy nursery? The nappy stage, crawling and first steps are exciting, demanding and vulnerable times – so too with the infant church plant.

The early life of the new church is a time of rapid change. It needs careful management. Much of the leaders' and team's task will shift away from vision towards management and administration. Questions like 'Who's going to put out the chairs next week?' seem to multiply. These are important issues and should not be despised. All the same it is important that leaders still recognize their visionary role. It is best to schedule more frequent meetings on nuts and bolts issues and to continue with periodic reviews of overall vision. Remember: the key shift at launch-time is from *task* to *people*.

Orientation for newcomers becomes a priority. New Christians need discipleship and building into the Christian faith as well as into this particular new community of believers. New members, whether they are new Christians or simply new to the congregation, need quickly to understand the church's vision.

We hope that all who plant churches will do so because they hear a call from God, and are ready to be guided by him in prayer and to get all the help they can form the experience of others.

BRIEFING 5

Birth and Beyond

Maturing a Plant
by George Lings

See **Resources** for details of this useful teaching tape addressing the down-to-earth issues of finance, annual meetings and accountability.

Be sure to restate the vision (purpose, priorities and values) clearly and regularly. One of the greatest areas of vulnerability for an infant church is caused by the different demands and expectations brought in by Christians from different backgrounds. It is helpful for *everyone* to go through an orientation course which includes the history and vision of the church as well as Christian basics.

The flood of demands from new people can easily make a church plant lose its emphasis on outreach. Resist that temptation and remember that 'new Christians win new Christians best'. As long as they are given simple guidance in being sensitive with their friends and family, they will be your best evangelism resource.

In this phase it is important to get new folk involved. Don't let them drift. As they are 'plugged in' they can get *ownership* of the church vision. Start by giving them undemanding jobs such as putting out chairs or making tea. But aim to develop them quickly into the next generation of leaders.

Adolescence – an identity crisis? All parents of teenagers know how adolescents react as they start searching for their identity with their peer group, rather than simply accepting it from their parents. A similar process is true in the life of the developing church plant. Knowing that this stage is likely to begin between two and four years after the launch, should help leaders anticipate problems and make necessary adjustments. In the infancy phase it was vitally important to steer a course based firmly on the original vision of the planting team, with no re-negotiation. With the coming of adolescence, it is time to step back and reassess.

The vision can now develop and change on the basis of:

- the history and experience of the church plant so far;
- the new people whom God has brought in, with all their gifts.

Adolescence is a time of growth and maturing, when the development of leadership is very important. It will be very helpful to have a strategy of delegation and second-level ministry in which apprentice leaders can learn safely as they are mentored.

New structures may be required to reflect greater independence from the parent church. This can be a problem area for church plants. Beware lest the description 'daughter church' leads to a permanent 'dependency syndrome' in the new church, or a resentment on the part of the 'mother' as the plant gains independence. From early on the level and timing of eventual independence needs to be communicated. The healthiest long-term aim may well be the achievement of a 'sister' relationship.

Prayer track

The birth of the church plant is likely to be a busy, exciting and stressful time. It's a time when the plant needs all the prayer support it can get – even though it seems as if there is no time to pray. Resolve like Bill Hybels, pastor of Willow Creek Community Church, to be *Too Busy Not To Pray* (the title of his recent book).

- Enlist as many people from the 'mother' church as possible to give concerted prayer support as you launch.
- Consider special prayer events prior to the launch such as a prayer vigil, a half night of prayer or a prayer concert.
- Some church plants have launched with a prayer carnival around their area, finishing up at the new venue for their first service.

Birth and Beyond

DISCUSSION 5

Discipleship and nurture

Notes

If your plant fulfils your plans and hopes, you will see new people being reached. Many of them will have no Christian faith, or will have lapsed from the church years ago. It is vital therefore to nurture these people to become strong Christians, committed to following Christ and being his church. In fact, taking Jesus' commission seriously requires making discipleship a central theme of all church life for all members.

There are many programmes and resources you can use in this process. To help you to choose the right ones or prepare your own approach, try the following exercises on your own or in your team, making notes of your conclusions.

1 'Go and make disciples...'

Reflect on your Christian development and consider who has had the biggest influence on your life and ministry. Ask yourself what factors were crucial in this person's effect on you.

- What have been the key element in your Christian growth?
- Was there anything lacking in the way your church responded to you?
- Do you feel that your church / group is providing for the needs of the new Christians among you at the moment?

2 'teaching them to obey...'

Jesus' words show that biblical discipleship is obedience-oriented, whereas the modern, Western approach is often knowledge-oriented.

- Try to assess the balance of the 'discipleship input' in your own life. How much is about developing understanding and knowledge, and how much is about doing and being – living out that knowledge. Is this the right balance?

3 'all that I have commanded you...' (Matthew 28:19,20)

Make a list of the commands Christ gave. Compare it with the list of broad categories below which were developed by George Patterson from his church planting experience. Read his story on page 39.

- Repent and believe
- Be baptized (and continue in the new life it initiates)
- Love God and neighbour in a practical way
- Celebrate the Lord's Supper
- Pray
- Give
- Disciple others

Do you think these commands form a good basis for nurturing and discipling new Christians?

Birth and Beyond

Mission impossible? A case study

Church planting is a perfect opportunity to explore new forms of worship. There are also many challenges to be faced connected with the building, musicians, leadership, sacraments, being outsider-friendly and so on. It becomes vitally important to decide what are the essential elements within a worship service. Try the following case study to get creativity flowing within the team.

Scenario: You are the lay leadership team of an Anglican church plant which has been running for about six months. You are meeting on Saturday evening to pray for the Communion Service tomorrow. Some new Christians from completely unchurched backgrounds have joined the congregation. Team members arrive at the meeting with a variety of tales of woe:

- The contractors building a new multi-screen cinema next to the building in which you meet have accidentally severed the power cables, making it impossible for you to use the OHP, the electric keyboard and other power-dependent musical instruments for leading worship. For the purposes of this exercise the season is Summer – and a warm one too!
- The only guitarist in the church has just returned from seeing his family in Scotland. He has left his acoustic guitar on the sleeper service from Glasgow. He won't be able to get it in time for tomorrow and no one knows of any other instruments you can borrow.
- The hymn books that you normally use are in the back of a team member's car which, as you meet, is probably being raced round a field or set alight in some woods as it was stolen earlier this afternoon and the police have not yet located it.
- The vicar from the parent church who was due to come and preside over the Communion, has contacted the group to apologize – he has come down with a very bad flu and cannot leave home.

You feel that it's too late to cancel the service and to let down the church, especially the new Christians. Your prayer meeting has therefore also become a planning meeting for the service. The service runs from 10.30 – 11.30 a.m.

Your task (should you wish to accept it) is to come up with a service plan to use tomorrow. Note down the different elements of the service fitting them into a time plan. Be as creative and flexible as you like. The chart divides the service into ten-minute blocks. Adapt this pattern to suit your plans.

Time	Activity	Leader
10:30 – 10:40		
10:40 – 10:50		
10:50 – 11:00		
11:00 – 11:10		
11:10 – 11:20		
11:20 – 11:30		

Birth and Beyond

Notes

The essentials

As a leadership team decide on what you would say are the essential elements in a worship service.

George Patterson, regarded by some as the father of the modern church planting movement, travelled to Honduras to teach in a seminary. On arrival, he found that it had been closed because it wasn't achieving its purpose of mobilizing village church leaders. 'You're promoted,' he was told by his supervisor, pointing to a mule and a smelly old saddle. 'Here is the Chair of Evangelism and Church Planting in the new Extension Evangelism Institute.'

Facing the challenge, George set about travelling through the villages of Honduras, discipling family leaders to plant their own churches. Citing our great commission to 'Go and make disciples of all nations... teaching them to obey all I have commanded you,' his principal emphasis was on the *commands of Christ*. As a result, over one hundred new churches were planted! Bearing in mind the simplicity of their circumstances, and his emphasis on Christ's commands, George arrived at seven essential elements for a worship service.

- Confession and absolution
- Praise
- Prayer
- Word (preaching and testimony)
- Giving
- Communion
- Fellowship

What do you think of these in comparison to your own list? Are there any which surprised you? How does it differ from your list?

Planting for growth: seven signs

Once a church plant is firmly established and is through both the birth and infancy stages, many of the principles for its healthy development are the same as for any local congregation. The Church Growth Movement, through many years of careful study, broadly agrees on the main factors that promote health and growth. Here are Peter Wagner's *Seven Signs*. Discuss these and decide early on how you will incorporate such principles in your church plant.

1. Dynamic, 'possibility-thinking' leader.
2. Well-mobilized laity.
3. Appropriately-sized venue: a building that is neither half empty, nor over eighty per cent full.
4. Right priorities.
5. Basically one kind of people: socially and culturally appropriate to the community.
6. Evangelistic method which works.
7. Celebration + congregation + cell. Each of the three levels of structure is present.

CPAS
Athena Drive
Tachbrook Park
WARWICK
CV34 6NG
Tel: 01926 334242
24hr Orderline: 01926 335855
Fax: 01926 337613

REFERENCE

Resources

Further resources from CPAS

1995 CPAS Code	*Title*	*Author and Publisher*
82001	**Creating Confidence in Evangelism**	John Young, CPAS
82002	**Practical Ideas in Evangelism**	John Young, CPAS
82003	**Creating a Church for the Unchurched**	Anne Hibbert, CPAS
00351	**Christian Basics**	CPAS video-based course
00501	**Growing Groups**	CPAS video-based course
85001	**The Gospel and Tomorrow's Culture**	Graham Cray, CPAS
86001	**Launching a Missionary Congregation**	Robert Warren, CPAS
03410	**Building Missionary Congregations**	Robert Warren, Church House Publishing
03577	**Church Planting: The Training Manual**	Martin Robinson and David Spriggs, Lynx
03404	**Church Planting: Models for Mission**	Bob Hopkins, Grove Booklets
82006	**Reaching Young Families**	Judith Wigley, CPAS
85003	**Unchurched People Welcome Here**	Rory Keegan, Paul Simmonds, Anne Hibbert, CPAS

Resources from ACPI

The following resources supplement the material in this workbook:

Anglican Church Planting Initiatives – services available (leaflet)

The Life-cycle of a Reproducing Church (booklet).

An example of an outline mission statement and planning framework for a new church.

Sample neighbourhood surveys.

Church Planting Stepwise implementation checklists.

Planting Unit Sizes and Keys to Success.

All of the above are available for the cost of photocopying and postage from Anglican Church Planting Initiatives, 38 Lascelles Street, St Helens, Merseyside WA9 1BA Tel: (01744) 758886

Also available from ACPI

Maturing a Plant by George Lings (teaching tape)

The Cramlington Story (video)

Also recommended

Sowing, Reaping and Keeping — Laurence Singlehurst, Crossway